Best wishes,

Mark Hamill

P. Hamill

tooth&claw
living alongside Britain's predators

PETER CAIRNS & MARK HAMBLIN

WHITTLES PUBLISHING

Published by
Whittles Publishing Limited
Dunbeath
Caithness
Scotland
KW6 6EY
United Kingdom
www.whittlespublishing.com

ISBN 978-1904445-46-3

Text and cover design by Iain Sarjeant

Printed by Polskabook

CONTENTS

INTRODUCTION

Our relationship with predators has always been fractious and they continue to court controversy as much today as at any time in Britain's history. For many people, predators are symbolic of a wildness we once knew, they are key to the ecological integrity of our countryside. They embrace notions of nobility and power. They make us feel good. For others, predators represent competition for our game interests and pose a threat to our domesticated animals. They are an inconvenient drain on resources and compromise our leisure pursuits – they have no place in our orderly lives where Man has dominion over nature.

Very few of us with an interest in the British countryside, remain indifferent about predators. We all have views on how, or whether, they should be managed. Our opinions are influenced by myth, culture, politics and economics. Emotion too plays its role and the fact that predators kill other animals in order to survive, can provoke extreme reactions in us.

So how does Britain really feel about its wild predators and do our attitudes towards these charismatic creatures afford us a window on our changing relationship with the natural world? These are some of the questions that *Tooth & Claw* sets out to answer.

During the course of our work, we have both met lots of different people involved with wildlife management and we have often discussed how fickle our relationship with other species has become. We are all selective to a lesser or greater degree. We make value-judgements on which species we like, where we think they should live and in what numbers. When it comes to predators, our views are also influenced by what they eat. When that impacts on us, no matter how insignificantly, few people can stand back and remain objective.

We wanted to explore those sensitive areas where predators and Man are coming into ever-closer contact and what this means to the people involved. How are perceptions shaped by occupation, upbringing, peer groups and ecological knowledge?

Over the past three years, we have spoken to a wide variety of individuals and organisations involved with predator management. We've also collected thousands of contributions via the *Tooth & Claw* website and had many more sent to us independently. Farmers, researchers, gamekeepers, conservationists, tourism operators – all of these and many others have livelihoods and interests that are influenced by how we perceive and react to our wild predators. Ultimately, we are all affected by predator-prey relationships. Predators are fundamental to the health of our ecosystems, helping to shape the landscape and the species that live within it. Us included.

Today's lifestyles have divorced many of us from the realities of the natural world. We consider ourselves managers of nature rather than participants. We live in a cosseted environment where we no longer need to compete with other predators for food. Thus, we are in danger of severing our link with other species. Increasingly, people perceive no need to interact with nature; it has become irrelevant in their lives and therefore has little value. Yet nature is not only relevant, it is an essential part of our well-being. A fox eating a rabbit may seem like an insignificant event but that one act is part of a much more complex set of biological processes, which enable our own species to thrive – to drink fresh water and breathe clean air.

In spite of the spectre of indifference, we have found that in the main, the British public cares deeply about its wildlife and that where there are conflicting views, there is a recognition that improved predator understanding and open dialogue can help ease tensions. There remain entrenched, self-motivated positions and ecologically inaccurate viewpoints but an increasing number of people recognise that our predator populations, many of which are expanding, are something to celebrate.

Public pressure has lead to more stringent protection for many of the species we previously persecuted and they are returning. But during their absence, habitats have changed and so have we. Our relationship with nature is now very different and although many of us like the notion of wildness and all that comes with it, we accept it only on our terms. Those terms often demand that predators do not impact on our carefully engineered lives. When they do, charity can be short-lived. At such times, we should not forget that we too are predators – by far and away the most efficient on the planet.

Throughout this project, we have remained impartial, considering our role as one of informing rather than persuading. We have adopted no political agenda and our objective has always been simply to improve understanding of predator-prey processes and to nurture empathy with different viewpoints surrounding predator-related issues.

In the long term, if we make the effort to put aside our prejudices and take the time to listen to the views of others, then more imaginative solutions may be found, which allow us to live harmoniously alongside healthy predator populations. In so doing, we have an opportunity to nurture a more ecologically rich environment for those who will inherit the consequences of our actions.

Peter Cairns and Mark Hamblin...with a great amount of help from you!

WHO'S AFRAID OF THE BIG BAD WOLF?

Once one of the most widely distributed land mammals on the planet, the wolf has long been subjected to systematic persecution at the hands of Man. But the winds of change are blowing for this apex predator which has long carried the burden of fear and hatred. The modern wolf has become an ambassador for a new conservation ethos that is challenging traditional perspectives throughout the developed world.

We reached the old wolf in time to watch a fierce green fire dying in her eyes. I realised then, and have known ever since, that there was something new to me in those eyes – something known only to her and the mountain. I was young then and full of trigger-itch; I thought that because fewer wolves meant more deer, that no wolves would mean hunter's paradise. But after seeing the green fire die, I sensed that neither the wolf nor the mountain agreed with such a view.

Aldo Leopold, forester, writer and spiritual leader, wrote these words in 1944 at a time when, following decades of predator killing across the United States, he and leading American scientists of the day were becoming increasingly assertive about the need to restore a place for wolves. Leopold was a pragmatic man, a friend once observing that his thinking was 'not that of an inspired genius but that of an ordinary fellow trying to put two and two together'. In spite of an early preoccupation with hunting large carnivores, Leopold's views changed and he committed himself to communicate to the American public why they should care about predators.

A century earlier, European colonists faced with the vastness of North America's rolling plains and endless forests, were reminded by puritan ministers of their Christian obligation to 'destroy that which is wild and make something of the land'. The ecological destruction that unfolded across America during the frontier days embraced an ideal that equated mountain lions, coyotes, wolves and bears with the work of Satan himself. No-one knows how many predators were killed during the 19th and early 20th centuries, but estimates run into millions. Between 1883 and 1918, 80,730 wolves were bountied in the state of Montana alone. Even forerunners of the American conservation movement had no time for wolves. In 1904, William Hornaday, hunter turned passionate conservationist, wrote: 'Of all the wild creatures in North America, none are more despicable than wolves. There is no depth of meanness, treachery or cruelty to which they do not cheerfully descend'.

The question that persisted in the American west from the very beginning of the pioneer years was one that nobody could answer: What good were wolves to anyone? Leopold was the first to craft a response: 'The last word in ignorance is the man who says of an animal or plant: What good is it? If the land mechanism as a whole is good, then every part is good, whether we understand it or not. Who but a fool would discard seemingly useless parts? To keep every cog and wheel is the first precaution of intelligent tinkering'.

America's onslaught on its wolves, though alarming, is by no means unique. Britain's countryside has been characterised by extensive and relentless 'vermin control' for longer than records exist and seemingly 'useless parts' have been dismantled and discarded since the arrival of Neolithic herdsmen. The embryo of what we now politely term 'wildlife management' was conceived long before Victorian sportsmen and gamekeepers launched their well-documented war on Britain's predators.

In a geological context, it is merely a blink of the eye since our tiny island was carpeted in a vast temperate forest where natural processes flowed uninterrupted and predator numbers were kept in check by climate, habitat and the availability of prey – a process of self-regulation. With the arrival of people and their changing needs, forests were felled for grazing pasture and game was hunted in increasing numbers: there was no place for competition from other species. Bears and lynx – both once widespread – had disappeared by the Middle Ages but the highly adaptable wolf clung on to a tenuous existence until the 18th century – eventually drowning in the symbolism that we laid at its door.

Not so long ago Britain's landscape was governed according to nature's rules.

For countless generations, the wolf has been the stuff of childhood nightmares. The root of our fear probably rests with tales of wolves eating people. Such stories are likely to have at least some probability, as over the centuries a growing human population ate into wolf habitat and reduced the availability of its natural prey. It is likely that desperation may well have compromised the wolf's natural fear of humans. In times of war, accounts of wolves gathering to feed on bloodied corpses and their tendency to exhume the dead, desecrating sacred ground, fuelled fear and hatred amongst God-fearing Christians.

A scene with obvious symbolism and instantly recognisable to generations of children.

All of Britain's predators have at one time or another, found themselves on the vermin hit list, justifiably or otherwise. However, it is unlikely that any were pursued with the same vigour as the wolf. After centuries of trying, Britain finally closed its door on *Canis lupus* when, according to legend, the hunter MacQueen presented the head of the last wolf in Scotland to the Laird of MacIntosh near Findhorn in Moray in 1743.

The motivations for eradicating the wolf in Britain and across much of its range were many and varied. It would be churlish to blame previous generations for their apparent disregard of nature's wealth. European colonists based their attitudes towards nature on what they read in the Bible: man was placed on this earth to have dominion over the rest of creation. The recognition that all life is interdependent and that even the wolf has its own ecological niche is a contemporary science and primarily the preserve of educated, affluent societies who can afford charity towards erstwhile competitors.

The Polson Stone which marks the killing of Sutherland's last wolf is tucked away in a lay-by at the side of the busy A9 trunk road.

TO MARK THE PLACE NEAR WHICH
(ACCORDING TO SCROPE'S "ART OF DEERSTALKING")
THE LAST WOLF IN SUTHERLAND
WAS KILLED
BY THE HUNTER POLSON,
IN OR ABOUT THE YEAR 1700,
THIS STONE WAS ERECTED BY
HIS GRACE THE DUKE OF PORTLAND, K.G.,
A.D. 1924.

For America's wolves, Leopold's insight came too late. By the time his innovative thinking gained credibility, the war on wolves was already won and the species had all but disappeared from the lower 48 states. But 100 years on from the height of wolf killing, events in America took a significant and symbolic turn when, in 1995, under the glare of the world's media spotlight, the ghost of the wolf conflict was finally laid to rest. Following decades of divisive debate, the American public voted to restore the wolf to parts of the Northern Rockies after an absence of 70 years. Dubbed as the most controversial feat of conservation in US history, the release of 31 Canadian wolves into Yellowstone, the world's first National Park, was globally scrutinised and sparked a renaissance in our appetite to see wolves restored elsewhere in their natural range. So how did a nation that spent most of its history ridding itself of wolves come to expend similar effort in returning them?

It has long been argued that a fundamental moral duty should be good enough reason to restore a species, which in less enlightened times we

Wolf watching has become big business. Yellowstone's wolves are reportedly worth $26m each year in tourism revenue.

eradicated by methods of baffling cruelty. However, it is rare for such a notion to hold any political weight and support must then rest on other motivations.

The return of wolves to Yellowstone was significant. For the very first time, scientists were handed the unique opportunity to study the ecological effects of restoring an apex predator to a largely intact ecosystem. When a wolf pack kills an elk, it will eat what it wants leaving the carcass for scavengers such as foxes, ravens and eagles. The carcass will then feed invertebrates before returning phosphorus and other nutrients to the soil. Soil that will then nourish fresh vegetation growth, which in turn will feed hungry herbivores. In Yellowstone, elk herds that previously concentrated in favoured grazing areas are now less inclined to remain static. This has allowed riparian growth including aspens, to return to river flood plains, creating insect-rich pools for fish and attracting beavers for the first time in decades. The return of wolves has thus released a series of effects far beyond the killing of its prey. Ecologically, the wolf has proved itself to be anything but a 'useless part'.

It is true to say that wolves are by no means universally popular in America: this is an animal that courts controversy and generates fear – no longer for the wolf itself but for the changes that their presence may bring about in the management of America's rural landscape. Ed Bangs, the man in charge of all wolf decisions in the Rocky Mountains, has said that the frenzy surrounding wolf restoration was so great it became clear to him how people had historically come to burn witches.

Everyone has an opinion about wolves but despite having become one of the most thoroughly studied animals on the planet, it remains widely misunderstood. How much of what we feel about the wolf – good and bad – is based on what we know of its biology? How many of us with an opinion can claim our views to be based on fact rather than anecdote? How easy is it therefore to make assumptions and generalisations which may nurture prejudice in others? And so it is with all predators. Much of what our predecessors believed was rooted in myth but current perspectives on predators are influenced by different factors, mostly driven by short-term self-interest.

After decades of dealing with irate ranchers bemoaning unacceptable, and often exaggerated levels of predation on their stock and wolf-loving urbanites who would have us all believe they can do no wrong, Ed Bangs has concluded: "People don't hate wolves; they hate what wolves symbolise. People don't love wolves; they love what they symbolise. The reality is always somewhere in between."

In Britain's increasingly material society, struggling to shrug off traditional notions of social division, our opinions on contemporary predator issues – fox hunting, cat ownership, raptor persecution and even the return of wolves – are governed more by socio-economics than they are by ecological considerations.

Within the context of our development, we have only very recently discovered a set of values that prioritise species protection and the manifestation of this, the modern conservation movement, has caught on very quickly. Against the backdrop of increasing concern over our impact on fragile ecosystems and finite natural resources, Britain has become a strong political voice, backed by public support, for the preservation of wildlife species.

Our hunting methods have changed beyond recognition. Freed from competition, and with our needs readily met, we can afford the luxury of charity to other species. Or so you might think.

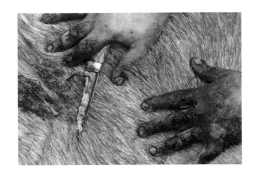

"MOST HUMAN MANAGEMENT OF OUR WILD ANIMALS IS FOR SELFISH PLEASURE AND GREED."

TOOTH & CLAW CONTRIBUTOR

This newly-found sympathy for nature has taken the more traditional outlook, which sees the land as a resource for exploitation, by surprise. The result in many instances is a battleground for a wide spectrum of single-interest agendas, all competing to influence the predator management process. Many such groups have become highly-skilled in filtering 'factual' information to the public to best serve their agenda. These 'facts' then form the basis for mainstream opinion with the gaps being filled in with cultural, social and economic influences. The result is that managing predators today is rarely about the animal itself – it is about managing people's perceptions – what we believe, what we value and how we perceive our dependency on nature. The return of wolves to the Rocky Mountains, although ecologically successful, will ultimately depend on human values.

"WE ARE THE PLANET'S TOP PREDATOR, AND IF WE CAN'T GIVE OTHER PREDATORS ROOM ON THIS INCREASINGLY MONEY-DRIVEN WORLD, THEN WE HAVE REACHED A SAD AND MORALLY REPREHENSIBLE STATE OF AFFAIRS."

TOOTH & CLAW CONTRIBUTOR

There is another factor, perhaps more serious than any political wranglings, which influences the value that future generations will place on nature: apathy. Shopping centres and retail parks are quickly becoming the hub of community life in modern Britain. Material wealth has become the barometer for how we measure 'success'. Natural play for our children is increasingly restricted to supervised, structured activities with few children afforded the freedom to discover nature through creative play thus denying them the opportunity to forge lifelong friendships with the forest or the meadow. It is not surprising then, that much of society – young people in particular – perceive no need to engage with nature. For those who do, virtual nature – that experienced in front of the television or computer screen – forms the foundation for their perceptions.

A busy high street scene mirrored the length and breadth of Britain reflects modern-day priorities and aspirations.

Amie is a typical 15-year-old and lives in the Midlands. She sports the latest designer summer wear and can text on her mobile at lightning speed without even looking. Her house is equipped with digital everything. She sits down on her sofa eating a bag of chicken crisps and gently strokes Tiger Lily, her pet tabby cat, that lies sprawled across the cushions. Amie is an animal lover and detests any form of what she sees as cruelty. "I hate fox hunting," she says emphatically. "It's just posh people with 15-bedroomed houses having fun. They have kids doing it and they grow up thinking it's right."

We talk about wolves. "If I knew there were wolves near where I lived, I wouldn't go out on my own, I wouldn't be allowed to!" We ask where this fear has come from. "It's on TV and in books like *Little Red Riding Hood*. In my mind, I know they would hurt me." We ask why other European countries should be expected to live with this threat. "It's different elsewhere," says Amie, "teenagers in countries like Sweden have grown up with wolves so they know how to live with them."

In Tayport on Scotland's east coast, Andrew Ford is studying to become a countryside ranger. He too is 15. "I'm the only one in my year who's interested in nature – most of the kids live in the middle of Dundee so very few experience what it's like to be in the countryside," he says.

Andy has been doing volunteer work at a local nature reserve. He has been helping to control crows, which involves either shooting or catching them in traps. "I have no problem with this," he says. "Crows have become very numerous – mainly because of us with landfills and takeaways on the streets. They impact on songbirds in a way that is not natural."

Andy's parents have always encouraged him to take an interest in nature and are keen birdwatchers themselves. Not all of his views are measured and reasoned however. "Cats are one thing I really hate – they're a non-natural predator and kill lots of birds. I'd happily shoot them if it was legal!"

Just a generation ago, this teenager might have spent his spare time climbing trees or building dens.

So what about wolves? Andy ponders. "It's a shame we have destroyed our wolves and they are no longer part of our culture but I'm not sure about having them back – I have a bit of a phobia about large predators. I saw a TV programme about a lion attacking a man in Africa – it almost tore his arm off and I've still got that image in my head."

Daniel is 16 and lives in St. Albans. The end of his summer holidays are approaching and for the past three days he has maintained a noon to night vigil on his computer, his bedroom curtains drawn, the lights on and the only interruption being the intermittent bleep of a text message on his mobile phone. Still in his pyjamas, he continues to tap methodically on the keyboard as we discuss the relevance of wildlife in his life. He thinks for a while, then responds. "I don't really care about it, I guess. It's not really important to me." We push him on how he sees his place in nature. "I don't know, I guess I haven't really thought about it." His mobile bleeps and we wait while he taps in a reply.

We ask him what he thinks about wolves. "Not a lot," he shrugs. "Aren't they nearly extinct in England?" Daniel's obvious indifference reveals little room in his technology-driven life for anything other than what immediately surrounds him.

Amie, Andrew and Daniel are not unusual. Their views are representative of many of tomorrow's decision-makers. Their perspectives reflect their individual backgrounds, upbringing and the myriad influences that shape their attitudes towards other species and other people.

"WE SHARE THIS PLANET...WE DO NOT OWN IT."
TOOTH & CLAW CONTRIBUTOR

Dr Alistair Bath is Associate Professor at Memorial University in Canada and is a current council member of the Large Carnivore Initiative for Europe. He has spent more than 25 years studying attitudes towards large predators and has long since concluded that conserving predators is a socio-political issue with solutions being achievable only by listening to all interest groups – including young people. "We're born with two ears and one mouth, so we should be listening at least twice as much as telling," he says.

In 2000, Alistair was commissioned by WWF(UK) to compile a report on the feelings of Britain's teenagers towards wolves and bears. Recognising that misconceptions based on mythology can create lasting impressions, the research wanted to encourage children, as future policy makers, to find out more about these apex predators. The average age of the 6,100 teenagers questioned was 13.

The report revealed an alarming lack of knowledge about both species but an overwhelming support for conserving them nonetheless. Perhaps surprisingly, while 61% of UK teenagers thought that it was important that wolves existed in Europe, their counterparts in Spain – in an area that is home to 2,000 wolves – expressed even more support (87%), bringing into question the assumption that those living alongside wolves are likely to be more negative towards their presence.

The report concluded that teenagers with greater knowledge of wolves and bears expressed much more positive attitudes towards them and that fear contributed to negative feelings. The survey also suggested that a loss of connection between young people and nature perpetuated both fear and misconceptions.

"WE HAVE TO LEARN TO SHARE THIS WORLD WITH OTHERS."

MONICA, AGED 11

It's a bright spring day in Combe, a sleepy affluent village in the heart of Oxfordshire. As the local primary children happily play tag during their lunch break, a trailer holding two adult wolves pulls up at the school gates. Several children run to the fence and excitedly whisper to each other. The wolves have come to town.

The UK Wolf Conservation Trust, a charity dedicated to conservation through education, has been invited to talk to the children about wolves. Once the children are quietly settled, Toni Shelbourne, the Trust's Senior Education Officer, starts her presentation. There are sighs of adoration when a picture of a week-old wolf cub is shown, quickly followed by cries of disgust as Toni explains how wolves often kill beavers and foxes. Toni is inundated with questions but is keen to show the children the real thing.

Outside in the playground, the children line up as Duma and Dakota, two socialised wolves, are walked in front of them. The two animals have seen it all before but the children are intrigued and chatter excitedly. Toni is asked about the biggest wolf, the fastest wolf and the most dangerous wolf. Even the teachers are keen to learn. In the background, five children watch from behind the classroom window, their parents having refused permission for them to be outside with the wolves present.

At the end of the afternoon, we ask one of the senior classes how many of them had been afraid of wolves at the start of the afternoon and were now less afraid. Twelve from the class of 30 raise their hands.

For more than a decade, those advocating wolf restoration in America devoted extensive educational resources to promote knowledge and awareness about wolf biology, something that ultimately provided the foundation for their return. Returning to the question of how wolves came to be restored to the Northern Rockies the answer is simple: because the majority of the American public wanted it.

Education packaged in a way that excites and engages young people is a powerful tool in nurturing understanding, knowledge and tolerance. This wolf doesn't know it but its visit may ignite a lifelong passion for wildlife in these young minds.

TOOTH & CLAW

Throughout human history, we have managed and manipulated wildlife populations to our own ends, playing the God-like role of deciding which species are allowed to prosper and those that are not. Wild animals – predators in particular – continue to be hostages to our attitudes. It is true to say that the wolf challenges the very core of our sense of control – something we worked very hard to establish. It is an animal that refuses to relinquish its wildness and to play by our rules. It is the antithesis of today's prescriptive countryside management. It is also a creature that is stirring the winds of change on behalf of all predators.

Here in Britain, we haven't had to answer difficult questions about wolves for three centuries but nevertheless, the issues surrounding today's predators are not so different. Whether we are willing to share our space with predators and to what extent, is a question that applies equally to the fox, the pine marten and the sea eagle as it does to the wolf.

Undoubtedly, predators touch our emotions on many levels. Aldo Leopold asked us: 'Who but a fool would discard seemingly useless parts?' The very survival of future generations may come to depend on the essential ecological services performed by countless 'parts' – all living organisms. The wolf, whatever we may feel about it, is one of those organisms.

"I'VE ALWAYS SAID THAT THE BEST WOLF HABITAT RESIDES IN THE HUMAN HEART."

ED BANGS

WHAT PRICE RURAL TRADITION?

Grouse shooting is woven into the fabric of rural life in much of upland Britain. The expansive carpets of heather on which red grouse depend may have romantic connotations but they are the stage for a cultural divide, where the impact of avian predators on grouse stocks is a subject for heated debate between rural traditionalists and raptor proponents.

It's July and without the luxury of a breeze, the midges are out in full force as we stomp through knee-high heather. A distant machine-gun like chatter pierces the breathless air and stops us in our tracks. Binoculars raised, we quickly pick out the distinctive white rump of the female hen harrier dive-bombing her more conspicuous silver-grey mate who is nonchalantly preening on a rocky outcrop. After several attempts to cajole him from his perch, she loses interest and we watch as she hovers over the rank heather then disappears as if the ground had swallowed her up. "She's brooding young chicks," asserts Brian Etheridge of the Scottish Raptor Monitoring Group. Brian has been ringing birds of prey in these remote Scottish glens for 40 years.

Meadow pipits provide melodious background music as we climb the steep hillside, the midges unrelenting. As we approach the nest site, we slow. Brian knows that the female harrier will sit tight as long as she dare and he wants to avoid any unnecessary stress. As we inch forward, she suddenly erupts from the heather filling the air with screeching alarm calls, swooping down with talons bared to warn us away. "She'll calm down in a few minutes," Brian assures us but in the meantime we keep a keen eye on her, as a protective harrier will think nothing of scraping her razor-sharp talons across our scalps.

On a flattened bed of vegetation, five small chicks huddle together, talons instinctively raised. "They look nice and healthy," beams Brian as he sets about weighing and measuring each one in turn. The nest is littered with prey remains – a golden plover, a few meadow pipits and a severed foot which Brian examines. "Red grouse," he confirms.

Watching the female safely back onto the nest from a distance, Brian is satisfied that all is well. "This is perfect harrier territory," he comments. "Plenty of nesting sites, lots of food and no hassle from gamekeepers." This final point is highly significant to many raptor enthusiasts, who believe that controlling gamekeeper persecution is the key to the long-term viability of hen harriers on Britain's upland moors.

Hen harriers are ambush hunters, built for agility rather than speed. Their slow, moth-like flight enables them to quarter diligently over open ground in search of rodents and ground-nesting birds. Red grouse are inextricably linked to the vast swathes of heather moorland that carpet upland Britain and its chicks are frequently prey for breeding harriers. But grouse is a prized quarry of another predator; one that considers his claim far more legitimate. Man.

Grouse shooting reached its zenith during the late 19th century, supporting entire rural communities. Upland estates employed an army of gamekeepers to dispatch with impunity any predator that might compromise grouse numbers. Hen harriers were close to the top of that list and by 1900 they were all but extinct across mainland Britain. With thousands of keepers drafted for the First World War, hen harriers and other 'vermin' were handed a lifeline but their resultant return during the latter half of the 20th century ignited a bitter division between traditional sporting interests and a modern-day public, which had found compassion for raptors.

A female hen harrier politely requesting her mate to find more food.

Grouse moors today remain the economic and cultural cornerstone of many rural areas, particularly in eastern Scotland and northern England. The figures are impressive. An estimated 1,600 grouse shooting providers entertain 47,000 guests each year. In the late 80s, it was estimated that almost 5,000 square kilometres of Britain's moorland was devoted to grouse shooting. But all is not well. Grouse bags have been falling for decades and the revenue on which many shooting estates have come to depend is no longer reliable. The possibility of driven grouse shooting becoming a thing of the past is palpably close for some estates and for those employed to produce a healthy harvest, the pressure is on. Every red grouse taken by a bird of

Which is more valuable – the red grouse or the hen harrier? It depends who you ask.

Predator control has always been an integral part of moorland management. Foxes, stoats, weasels and corvids can all legally be controlled in Britain.

prey is seen as another nail in the coffin and it is unsurprising that some will go to extreme lengths to preserve their way of life.

Brian Etheridge looks out over the moor which stretches beyond every horizon. "I've been monitoring birds of prey most of my years and persecution is still as rife as ever," he sighs. "Some keepers use spotlights at night to shoot the female harrier – it's easy. Young keepers can be the worst of all – they've got 30 years ahead of them and feel they've a point to prove." Brian's frustration is clear. He has seen too many harriers, peregrines and golden eagles shot, poisoned or deliberately disturbed.

Adam Smith is Senior Scientist with the Game Conservancy Trust (GCT) in the Cairngorms. "With 20,000 acres of nothing around them, keepers have little fear of being caught. Some would rather risk prison than see the collapse of their moor," he tells us.

The GCT has 22,000 members and its objective is 'conservation through wise use'. Adam concedes that some members are 'just guns' but others have a broader perspective and the organisation does not encourage shooting in ignorance. "The upkeep of a moor is modelled on a three-legged stool," he continues, "habitat, disease and predator management. You cannot carry out any one of these in isolation."

All birds of prey in England, Scotland and Wales are protected under the Wildlife and Countryside Act 1981, and in Northern Ireland, The Wildlife (Northern Ireland) Order 1985. Following recent amendments to related legislation, sentencing options for crimes against wildlife now include imprisonment. The stakes are high.

In spite of the personal risk and growing public dismay over raptor persecution, the statistics are grim. In 2004, a survey indicated that Britain's hen harrier population had risen to 749 pairs (from 521 pairs

"KEEPERS LOCATE THE NEST DURING THE DAY THEN USE SPOTLIGHTS AT NIGHT TO SHOOT THE FEMALE – IT'S EASY."

in 1998), but that there had been significant decreases in areas with a concentration of shooting estates. Scotland experiences a disproportionate amount of the known killing and according to Alan Smailes, Divisional Commander of Grampian Police: "There is clear and persistent evidence of illegal persecution on some grouse moors."

Of the defendants convicted of offences relating to raptor persecution since 1980, over 80% were involved with shooting and most of these were gamekeepers. That birds of prey are being illegally killed is

Not everyone is pleased about a nationwide increase in raptor numbers. Scavengers such as red kites and buzzards are susceptible to illegal poisoning.

Golden eagles hunt ptarmigan and mountain hare in Scotland's uplands but will happily help themselves to red grouse given the chance.

beyond question. Given the remote nature of the terrain, the full extent of the problem is impossible to quantify but senior managers at RSPB Scotland are in no doubt that persecution is widespread and have reams of research literature to back up their assertions.

Keith Morton is one of RSPB Scotland's Species Policy Officers but is quick to point out that, "twenty years, 3 months and 18 days" of his career was spent with RSPB Investigations! Keith sits back in his chair and looks out of his Edinburgh office. "In the last 20 years, persecution has drastically reduced – you only have to look at the explosion in buzzards. It is highly significant that these days, very few within the farming community poison raptors but the problem is retreating uphill onto the grouse moors and is now down to a hardcore of persecutors – almost all of those will be gamekeepers."

Keith is weary of a battle in which he's been involved much of his life. "Some keepers simply cannot stop killing raptors – they just hate them. They might be told not to by their employer but they can't help themselves. Equally, there are keepers who do not like killing birds of prey but they have their bosses on their backs pressurising them."

Jerry Wilson, Head of Research for RSPB Scotland passes over a handful of reports documenting every facet of raptor persecution in recent years. It is apparent that the RSPB take this issue extremely seriously. "What is puzzling is that many keepers claim they cannot run their moors without killing birds of prey," says Jerry. "Surely this brings into question the whole viability of driven grouse shooting. There are perhaps a handful of moors in Scotland that make a small profit but these estates eliminate anything that competes with grouse – not only raptors but hares, sheep and deer."

Keith intervenes: "From an ecological point of view, I'm actually less concerned about harriers than you might imagine. They have a serious problem in England where breeding figures are critically low but the problem is simple: people are killing them. Stop killing them and harriers will quickly recover. I'm actually more concerned about golden eagles. If we started to see a significant decline in eagles, it

"Some keepers simply cannot stop killing raptors – they just hate them. They might be told not to by their employer but they can't help themselves."

would be much more difficult to bring them back because they breed so slowly. I can live with a certain amount of harrier persecution – it will stop eventually – but I am concerned about eagles."

In 2006, two golden eagles were found poisoned in the Cairngorms National Park and for the first time a substantial reward was offered for information leading to a conviction. One of the eagles was found on Glenfeshie, an estate often referred to as the 'jewel in the Cairngorms crown'. Thomas MacDonnell is the estate factor and is dismayed over the treatment his staff received during the initial investigation. "I was a firm supporter of the RSPB and allowed them full access to the estate but not now. They were not interested in asking us for help but instead fed stories to the media indirectly accusing us of the offence. This gave the public the impression that Glenfeshie is persecuting raptors and this is most definitely not the case."

It is apparent that the killing of birds of prey, hen harriers in particular, is not simply a matter of economics. A complex web of social and cultural influences which touches the very core of life on these upland moors determines the fate of each nesting attempt. It would appear that whilst persecution is widely condemned even within the game shooting industry, a persistent minority consider it not only justified but beneficial to wildlife conservation. So are there any quick-fix solutions? The RSPB holds onto the belief that 'improved law enforcement is the key to reducing wildlife crime'. But does such a hard line tackle the root of an entrenched resistance to change and a perception that conservationists are out to impose their will on a reluctant countryside and its people?

It's a warm summer's day on Royal Deeside in north-east Scotland and the breeze blows the bubbling calls of curlew across the moor. The patchwork quilt effect of the heather cloaks this entire upland lndscape. This is Scotland's Big Sky country. This is also grouse shooting central. In a couple of months, this wild moorland will be a blaze of vibrant purple hues as the heather bursts into flower. Local shooting estates are readying themselves for mid-August when the 'glorious 12th' signals the start of the annual grouse harvest. It is easy to understand the lure of these hills where the tapestry of subtle colours combines with an intoxicating cocktail of sounds and smells carried on the wind. This is a place where your senses are under assault.

The sight of a police car on these moorland roads is somewhat incongruous. David MacKinnon is Grampian Police's first full-time Wildlife Liaison Officer. He has an honours degree in agriculture from Aberdeen University and a lifelong interest in wildlife. A native to these parts, he's no stranger to the eclectic demands put on the Scottish countryside. "My job is simple because I'm impartial. I'm not anti-shooting and I understand that keepers have controlled pine martens, wildcats and raptors for centuries but these species are now protected and keepering practices must change. Those that choose to break the law must understand that they will be punished."

David has travelled over from Aberdeen as a representative of the North-East Raptor Watch, a partnership between Grampian Police, RSPB, Scottish Natural Heritage and the Cairngorms National Park Authority. The initiative is a three-year project to address the conflict between birds of prey and shooting estates. David has meetings arranged with several local estates to forge links and nurture support for the project. "The take-up has generally been very good," he tells us, "but there are a couple of estates we'd really like to get on board."

The figures for hen harriers in this region are startling. In 2004, Grampian held only 65 pairs – a 59% decrease since a previous count 20 years ago. Furthermore, research suggests that the density of breeding golden eagles, relative to suitable habitat, is also lower in Grampian than anywhere else in Scotland.

"In all honesty," continues David, "we're at rock bottom with persecution. Economics, peer pressure and cultural tradition all point to not having 'hooked beaks' on grouse moors and keepers also feel victimised. Their whole livelihoods are tied to their jobs and understandably they are defensive towards anything that threatens that. But the writing is on the wall and many know that wildlife legislation is only likely to become more onerous."

The wind gets up and large cumulus clouds bloom on the horizon. We retire to a local café where we're joined by Jim Craib, a local raptor enthusiast. Jim is another veteran of the harrier debate. His finger presses hard on the table. "On one estate I had the contents of three nests destroyed. Beside one we found the wing tags of a young harrier tied to the heather with the letters UU. We took this as a personal message: 'Up yours'. To some keepers, raptors are just weeds in the garden."

The situation seems intractable. Collaborative initiatives like the Raptor Watch and Operation Artemis, established in 2004 to specifically address hen harrier crime, are supported by a wide range of countryside interest groups but meanwhile, the killing continues with an estimated 11–15% of the Scottish mainland harrier population destroyed each year. In England between 1997 and 2002, no harriers successfully nested on managed grouse moors despite increases elsewhere.

David MacKinnon might understand keepers problems but his job is to enforce the law which protects all Britain's birds of prey.

Having keepered in Angus for 42 years, Bert Burnett is well attuned to the politics of what he describes as 'the raptor problem'. A burly, bearded man with penetrating eyes, Bert wears his heart on his sleeve. "Yes, there are keepers who kill raptors and I cannot condone that but they're frustrated at not being able to protect their stock – anybody would be. The conservationists want predator protection at any cost. Keepers don't want to eradicate predators – they just want some flexibility to allow them to do their job."

Bert Burnett is an old-school gamekeeper who sees his profession threatened and his colleagues unfairly victimised.

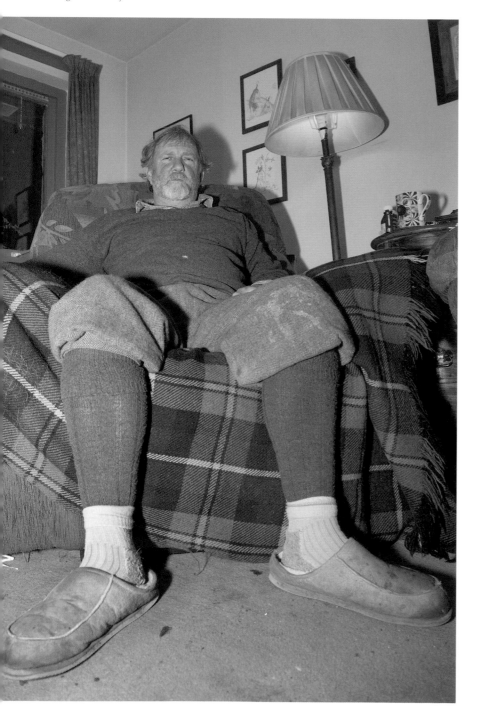

The flexibility to which Bert refers is a change in the law to allow control of avian predators where they impinge on shooting interests. He recommends a quota system whereby an upper limit is placed on the number of breeding raptors in a game shooting area. For species like buzzards and sparrowhawks, which are not deemed to be threatened, birds above the set quota would be culled. For less numerous species like hen harriers or red kites, the nests could be taken and the eggs hatched elsewhere. The adults could then be live trapped and relocated to areas where raptors are accepted. Such measures would require a derogation under the EU Birds Directive.

Outside Bert's cottage, the bird table is alive with activity – tits and finches all clamouring to feed. Bert continues: "Ten years from now, if the RSPB and the like have their way, we'll all be out of jobs. If keepering does continue, it'll be politically incorrect to call it that – we'll be land managers or wildlife rangers. That's bullshit. Keepers are a proud and often obstinate bunch and if the conservationists keep hitting us with a stick, they can go to hell – it does more harm than good. The only way I can see progress is if the RSPB and the like start talking sensibly to us." The sentiment is heartfelt.

"IF THE CONSERVATIONISTS KEEP HITTING US WITH A STICK, THEY CAN GO TO HELL."

Empathy for Bert's viewpoint comes from a surprising source. For 25 years, Mike Groves has been a hen harrier addict. Like a teenager fixated on a pop hero, he has accumulated piles of research papers and newspaper articles on this bird. For Mike, the hen harrier is the ultimate raptor pin-up. "They're just fantastic birds," he enthuses. For the last ten years, Mike has been a member of the Tayside Raptor Study Group and laments the general attitude towards gamekeepers.

"When I joined the group, there was an accepted ethos that we shouldn't talk to gamekeepers," Mike tells us. "When I had to, I spoke to them like they were second-class citizens." Mike clearly looks back on this time uncomfortably. "My perspective has changed. I decided to try and see things from their side of the fence and in doing so, I've built up good relationships with most of the keepers I work with – it's based on mutual respect. Many keepers now ring me and tell me about raptors they've seen on the moors – this is how it should be. I listen to these men, I talk to them and I can see their problems."

Mike shuffles in his seat. "What makes me really angry is the lack of progress. There should be 20–30 pairs of harriers in Angus – this year only one pair was successful. The system as it stands is failing and some common sense needs to prevail – we need to break down some barriers. It is obvious to me that five or six pairs of harriers on a grouse moor are not viable. Two pairs on 50,000 acres might be tolerated but keepers think that if they accept one pair, they'll be asked to tolerate ten. Sadly, it's also become a matter of principle in some areas. The hatred for certain conservation bodies is phenomenal and the harriers suffer."

"HARRIERS ARE FANTASTIC BIRDS, I'M ADDICTED TO THEM."

Mike's pragmatism has made him unpopular with his contemporaries who, he says, take a more conservative view. "Some of them can see what I see but they won't stand up and say anything." Like most individuals embroiled in this protracted and divisive issue, Mike is clearly fatigued by what he sees as obstinacy on the part of those in a position to change the fortunes of hen harriers.

He continues, "There are probably around 20% of estates that simply won't talk about raptors but the majority would be happy to discuss imaginative options like a quota system involving non-lethal control. At the moment it is a one-way process. The estates feel they give and give but get nothing back. This tension helps nobody, least of all hen harriers."

Presently, there are a number of legal options available to grouse moor owners to mitigate predation from upland raptors. Research suggests that providing alternative food for hen harriers during the breeding season in the form of dead rats or chicks can reduce grouse predation by up to 86%. In some areas, financial incentives are in place – up to £900 per nest per year – to encourage estates to adopt this technique.

RSPB's Jerry Wilson is disappointed in the take-up for diversionary feeding. "We've yet to find an estate that is willing to even experiment. Their attitude is predator control, that's what we do."

The culture behind predator management on shooting estates is complex and is rooted more in tradition than in ecological science. In some cases, it is clearly not so much the hen harrier that is the perceived enemy but those who seek to protect it. It has been suggested that the core issue is more to do with what our moorlands should look like and more importantly, who should control them.

The science of the relationship between red grouse populations and upland raptors came to a head in the mid-90s with the publication of the results from the Joint Raptor Study (JRS). This five-year project, undertaken by the Centre for Ecology and Hydrology and the Game Conservancy Trust, was funded to establish whether driven grouse shooting could retain viability in the presence of freely breeding raptors. The research focused on a grouse moor at Langholm in Dumfries & Galloway. The findings, published in 1997, have courted controversy ever since with varying interpretations being adopted by different single-interest groups.

Putting out alternative food for hen harriers can greatly reduce the pressure on grouse but this means time and effort and there seems little appetite to change traditional management practices.

During the research period, all breeding raptors were protected and their numbers quickly increased, clearly demonstrating previously high levels of persecution according to raptor proponents. Relieved from human interference, breeding peregrines doubled in the study period and harriers increased from two to fourteen pairs.

The study found that the subsequent predation on grouse accounted for a 50% decline in autumn stocks and shooting was suspended with the redeployment of keepering staff. It was widely accepted by many of the organisations involved that the rapid increase in raptor numbers, harriers in particular, had been largely responsible for the collapse in Langholm's grouse stocks and the cessation of shooting.

The RSPB and other conservation bodies have argued that birds of prey cannot be blamed for the long-term reduction of grouse bags. They have pointed out that harrier numbers increased only after 1990 but red grouse numbers had been falling for decades. It is also recognised that the impact of upland raptors on red grouse should be measured against various factors including the prolonged reduction in heather cover due to overgrazing. At Langholm, this was reported at 48% between 1948 and 1988, resulting in an annual 3% decline in grouse numbers. A link between prolonged loss of heather coinciding with an increase in sheep numbers and reducing grouse populations, has been strongly suggested for a wide range of moors across Britain's uplands.

The legacy of what is now referred to as 'The Langholm Debate' is a frustrating gulf in the interpretations adopted from the research by different interest groups. Subsequent research suggests that both meadow pipits and field voles – favoured prey items for hen harriers – are most abundant where there is a mosaic of both grassland and heather. It is plausible therefore, that a shooting moor that has lost heather due to grazing pressure will attract greater numbers of pipits and voles which in turn will attract generalist predators like harriers. This may then limit grouse productivity through increased predation.

Both the Game Conservancy Trust and The Heather Trust, an independent charity dedicated to the promotion of high standards of

By burning patches of rank heather in late winter, thus creating the familiar patchwork of vegetation at different growth stages, nutritious fresh shoots are provided for grouse alongside safe nesting habitat.

moorland management, attribute long-term grouse declines to the deterioration of heather management, disease and increased predation by foxes and crows. It is reported that between the 1940s and 1980s in Scotland alone, 4,165 square kilometres of heather cover was lost. The increase in grazing pressure that is widely blamed for deteriorating habitat is also supported by a doubling of the sheep population to 40 million between 1950 and 1990.

If improved habitat management is indeed fundamental to achieving a sustainable recovery of red grouse, this is clearly neither quick nor cheap. In the short term, the question on everyone's lips is: can a driven grouse moor remain viable in the presence of unchecked raptor numbers? Most people involved with commercial grouse shooting would argue not and in the presence of other pressures such as tick-borne disease, the impact of raptor predation is perceived as more pronounced. Solutions that are acceptable to a wide range of interests are hard to come by.

EU legislation presently excludes the possibility for controlling birds of prey unless all legal alternatives have been explored and found to be unsatisfactory. Those who support continued raptor protection contest that no effort has been put into exercising established techniques such as diversionary feeding and that grouse-raptor coexistence relies on long-term habitat improvements. Meanwhile, in the face of increasingly negative publicity, many keepers are unwilling to compromise. Positions remain entrenched.

The debate over how we marry a legitimate countryside pursuit with our newly-found appetite for re-establishing suppressed raptor species is complex. The familiar arguments are mirrored in comparable discussions over other species. Predators clearly mean different things to different people. To what degree they should be 'allowed' to impinge on human interests reflects the challenge of reconciling the widening chasm in our relationship with nature. Presently this conflict, perhaps more than most others, is characterised by those who choose to thump their chests and draw lines in the sand, an approach that has yielded little progress over a prolonged period. But there is room for optimism. A new research project is planned for Langholm and discussion forums in both Scotland and England provide an opportunity to explore different attitudes and perceptions amongst stakeholder interests. The challenge is surely to change what the hen harrier, the peregrine and the golden eagle represent to different interests. This can only be achieved by a coming together of those genuinely committed to finding innovative solutions and a recognition that science and legislation alone will not ensure a long-term coexistence with predators like hen harriers. People will do that.

EAGLE ISLAND

THE RETURN OF THE EAGLE
WITH THE SUNLIT EYE

Thirty years on from its reintroduction onto Scotland's remote west coast, the majestic sea eagle has risen to celebrity status on the Hebridean island of Mull.

TOOTH & CLAW

The morning air is still and all is silent as our small boat rocks gently on the mirror-calm fjord. Towering high above us the dark granite cliff is caressed in shafting sunlight, but reveals no sign of life. Then quietly, a deep, deliberate Norwegian voice proclaims "She is coming." Any movement is discernible only to the trained eye but the owner of the voice, Ole Martin Dahle, has such an eye. He knows these birds well and knows that the approaching eagle is a female lured from her clifftop nest by the temptation of an easy meal.

Seconds tick by but she remains unseen by the group of expectant eagle watchers. Suddenly, the unmistakable silhouette of Europe's largest raptor breaks the skyline. With no effort at all she is directly above us, weighing up her desire to feed two hungry chicks against the risk of entering a dive so close to our boat. Turning her sunlit eye briefly in our direction, she gauges the wind direction and makes her decision.

With an instant tuck of one wing she is corkscrewing earthwards, her focus now locked firmly on her prize. Ten metres above the water she lowers her bright yellow legs equipped with feet the size of a human hand, like an aircraft approaching a runway. The wind courses through her feathers as she spreads her white tail and holds up her wings to cut speed. She is now alongside the boat and with an outstretched talon deftly plucks the fish from the surface with barely a ripple.

A minute later she is back at her nest – a shambolic pile of twigs – feeding two young eaglets. The smile on the sun-reddened face of our Norwegian guide says it all, although one member of our group is even more elated and announces: "That was better than sex!" The Havörn, the white-tailed eagle, has cast her magic.

Ole Martin Dahle is an instantly likeable Norwegian farmer with honest eyes and a firm handshake. Born in Lauvsnes in Nord-Trondelag, a small fishing village connected by road to the rest of the country only 40 years ago, he has never moved from this rural

Bountiful Norwegian waters offer rich pickings for eagles and humans alike.

community. In Norwegian tradition, as the eldest son, he inherited the family farmstead. In a rapidly changing agricultural climate however, he reluctantly concluded that farming could not provide for himself and his young family. He now works part-time digging graves and mending roads but his passion – and an increasing amount of his income – is from his wildlife tourism business, *Norway Nature*. The thriving local white-tailed or 'sea' eagles are his trump card.

Ole Martin Dahle, a modern-day Viking!

"People think I am crazy," he laughs, "but they are starting to see the potential of this type of tourism. It is important to me that the community supports what I am doing and benefits from it." He pushes a piece of rolled up *snus* (tobacco) under his top lip and looks out to sea. "If the eagles become more valued through their economic potential, then my sons and their children can enjoy what nature has given to me."

There is no doubt that the experience of such an intimate encounter with a large and powerful bird of prey leaves a lasting impression. Ole Martin's growing number of guests from all over Europe are hungry for more and some have visited more than ten times in the last three years. In co-operation with local farmers and forest owners, hides have been built to photograph the eagles in winter and there is even talk about building a wildlife visitor centre in Lauvsnes – heady stuff for a village of only 600 inhabitants.

How times have changed. Fifty years ago, these opportunistic predators were being systematically persecuted with a bounty payable for each bird killed. They were accused of everything from sheep predation to child kidnapping and their numbers plummeted to around 600 pairs. In 1970, international pressure forced a change in the law and slowly, public attitude mellowed towards the eagles. Ironically, it took a sheep farmer to realise the financial opportunity these birds presented. Today, the sea eagle is once again a regular sight throughout Norway with an estimated 2,000 pairs taking advantage of the rugged coastline and bountiful waters.

This turnaround in fortunes for Norway's sea eagles coincided with the beginning of a roller coaster ride for the species 1,000 miles away on Scotland's west coast. In 1975, Norway provided the donor population for the return of these birds to the Highlands after an absence of nearly 60 years. Since then, 140 young eaglets have been translocated from

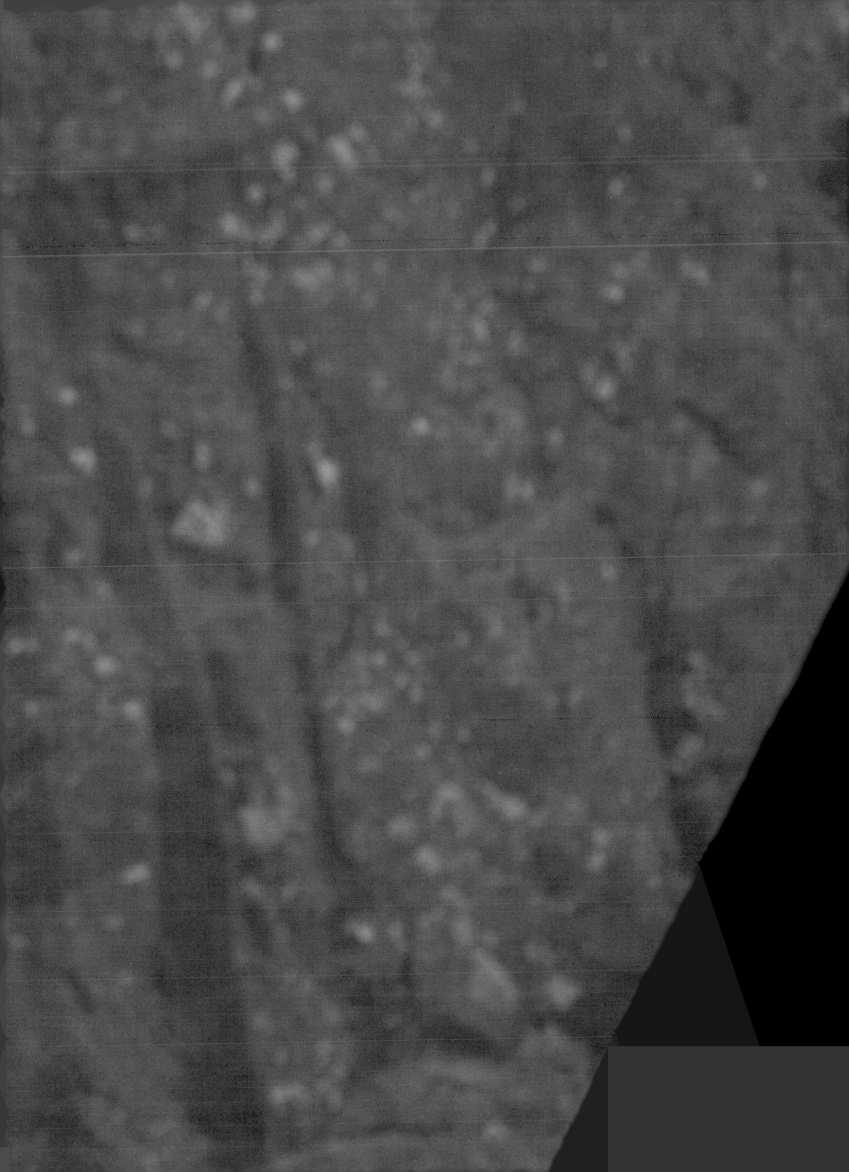

The rugged landscape of Mull supports Britain's highest density of breeding sea eagles.

Norway and the population in Scotland has slowly regained a foothold – the first chick fledged from a Scottish nest in 1985.

With around 35 pairs now occupying territory, the birds are established but they remain vulnerable. Theft of their eggs and illegal poisoning continues to be a threat and they remain susceptible to poor breeding success through bad weather. Their choice of prey also makes them unpopular with some land managers and farmers but the story of *iolair suil na greine* – the eagle with the sunlit eye – and their struggle to regain their historical range, has captured imaginations throughout the country.

"IT IS IMPORTANT TO ME THAT THE COMMUNITY SUPPORTS WHAT I AM DOING AND BENEFITS FROM IT."

On the Hebridean island of Mull it's early May and panic reigns as the late afternoon ferry approaches Craignure from Oban. Rows of coaches are lined up to take day-trippers back to the mainland but the souvenir-hungry visitors are packed into the Tourist Information Centre frantically buying books, postcards and tartan tea towels to remind them of their day on Mull. "It's the same every day," reports Maureen Dehany, the centre's manageress. "Why do they leave it all to the last minute?"

Following a brief respite, her extensive knowledge of the island is challenged for the umpteenth time today. A middle-aged couple want to know where they might see otters and sea eagles. Maureen gets out the map. She suggests they might benefit from a day out with one of the island's wildlife safari operators. After a lengthy period on the phone, she returns with a sullen expression – they are all booked for the week. The couple look disappointed but Maureen, always eager to help, offers to book them a place in the Loch Frisa viewing hide, the only facility in the world which looks directly onto a sea eagle nest. After several attempts, she reports the lines are engaged. The couple vow to return tomorrow to try their luck.

"This is becoming a regular occurrence," reports Maureen. "Until recently, most visitors headed straight to Tobermory (the filming location for a popular children's TV series) but now, people are coming to see the wildlife, especially the eagles."

Wildlife watching has become a major contributor to Mull's tourism economy.

A recent TV wildlife documentary beamed pictures of a sea eagle nest containing two chicks – nicknamed Itchy and Scratchy – into millions of homes across Britain. Since then, Mull's resident eagles have become local celebrities and the principal attraction for an increasing number of wildlife tourists. "It's great from our point of view," adds Maureen, "as visitors are now spread out across the island and more of our businesses get a slice of the cake."

The following day, a howling wind and driving rain make progress slow as we wind our way around the single track road towards Salen on Mull's east coast. Any eagle in its right mind will be keeping a low profile today. A Land Rover pulls into the car park and the smiling face of David Sexton, RSPB Scotland's Mull Officer, offers his hand and quickly suggests retreating to his home for coffee rather than battling our way through the forest to watch eagles.

Visitors to Mull are left in no doubt about the value placed on the island's eagles.

David saw his first sea eagle on Mull in 1980 and has followed the fortunes of the population ever since. "The response to the public hide at Loch Frisa has been overwhelming," beams David. "We had 3,500 visitors in 2005 and this year it is set to rise again." The revenue from the hide is split between the eagle project itself and the Mull & Iona Community Trust which funds a range of initiatives for local people, especially children.

All around Mull, there are conspicuous yellow signs promoting the Mull Eagle Watch, a unique initiative between islanders, Strathclyde Police, the RSPB and Forestry Commission Scotland. The main objective of the project is to prevent vulnerable sea eagle nests being targeted by egg thieves. Tracking egg thieves has become a sophisticated business and police intelligence has been invaluable in monitoring known collectors. Happily, they report no egg theft on the island since the year 2000.

David adds, "Ironically it was egg theft that acted as a catalyst to opening the Loch Frisa nest site to public viewing. Our logic was that the more eyes and ears of people taking note of suspicious activity, the better protected the site." Mull Eagle Watch presently has 45 volunteers with more wanting to get involved. The Loch Frisa site is watched 24 hours a day during egg incubation and for some this means night after night of interrupted sleep in a wooden shed – it's tough loving eagles!

"VISITORS ARE NOW SPREAD OUT ACROSS THE ISLAND AND MORE OF OUR BUSINESSES GET A SLICE OF THE CAKE."

In spite of the booming popularity of Mull's sea eagles and the economic benefits they bring, David acknowledges that not everyone is pleased to have these powerful predators back. "You don't have to scratch too far beneath the surface to find anti-eagle sentiment," he says. "This was not helped by the negative media coverage during the

90s with endless stories about lamb predation. Things have improved enormously since then but there will always be islanders who would prefer the birds not to be here." David understands this point of view but counters, "The economic benefits – now estimated at around £1.7m each year – are now starting to outweigh any problems that the eagles might create."

Those problems centre around widespread sheep farming on Mull with the inevitable temptation of newborn lambs in spring. In one event, an angry farmer personally handed David the bloodied carcass of a lamb, allegedly predated by a sea eagle. There are no foxes on the island and the local shepherds have had plenty of time to get used to life without large predators – that is until sea eagles returned.

"If you ask a farmer if he's happy about a metre-high raptor with a nine foot wingspan sat in his field, you'll get an interesting reaction," says Euan Warnock, Secretary of the local National Farmers Union for Scotland. "There are obviously economic factors that influence farmers' perspectives on sea eagles but there is also an emotional reaction. Some farmers have had eagles nesting on their land for 20 years now – that's 20 years of hassle, stress and financial loss, especially if those birds are habitual lamb hunters."

Although around a third of farmers on Mull have extended their businesses into tourism, there remain many whose livelihoods are dependent on sheep farming. Through Scottish Natural Heritage's (SNH) Natural Care scheme, there are now incentives for Mull's farmers to look out for both white-tailed and golden eagles who either nest or regularly hunt over their land. "Three or four years ago," Euan continues, "if you'd given farmers the choice between compensation and no eagles, the answer would have been unanimous. They felt they were given no respect and their feelings towards the eagles and conservation bodies in general, were verging on militant."

The disillusionment felt by many farmers over lamb predation can perhaps be traced back to the complete absence of any consultation about bringing these birds back in the first place. There was no

"If you ask a farmer if he's happy about a metre-high predator with a nine-foot wingspan sat in his field, you'll get an interesting reaction."

discussion with the rural communities that were being asked to live alongside these predatory birds. Once it became clear that sea eagles were predating lambs, the antagonism inevitably became more acute.

It appears there has been a general softening in anti-eagle feeling over recent years. The new scheme encourages positive management and some landowners qualify for payments of up to £5,000 each year for 'eagle wardening' and improved sheep management. "Working relationships with the likes of SNH have improved and farmers are openly less militant. It has a lot to do with respect," confirms Euan.

Before the Natural Care scheme, farmers were paid compensation for predated lambs. According to David Sexton, it was an unsatisfactory situation. "The process was lengthy and expensive," he says. "Carcasses had to be sent away for analysis before compensation could be paid and the farmer might not always have got the answer he wanted." David looks out of the window, the hostile weather and the effect on the eagles, clearly on his mind. "We are light years away from where we were ten years ago and the future is bright for the sea eagles on Mull. There is a healthy pool of unattached birds giving plenty of potential for future breeding. This should also be good news for the people on the island."

In spite of his optimism, David remains sensitive to anti-eagle feeling. In *Am Muileach* Mull's monthly newspaper, an anonymous letter appeared in March 2005, providing a stark reminder of antipathy towards eagles and a misguided understanding of predator biology.

The eagle will disable its prey by landing on its head or shoulders and digging in its talons. The sheep will then bolt in a panic often landing in a ditch or over a cliff where it will break a leg. A large animal is then at the eagle's mercy. The sea eagle then proceeds to a skilful piece of butchery, disembowelling the animal alive, taking its kidney or liver to its young. The eagle then returns at its leisure to feast on the remains of the live animal until it eventually dies.

This type of emotive account can easily influence people's perceptions of large predators like sea eagles. To establish whether such accounts and those of farmers claiming high levels of lamb predation hold water, the Scottish Executive commissioned research into this very issue between 1999 and 2002.

Sea eagles are generalist predators and scavengers. Their diet includes prey as diverse as rabbit, toad, octopus and seabirds. Monitoring and analysing food remains at remote eagle nests is therefore an inherently difficult job and can never claim to be an exact science. Although sea eagles are known to predate lambs, it was unclear whether this was having a financial impact for Mull's sheep farmers.

The research confirmed that in addition to scavenging dead lambs, Mull's sea eagles do also kill live lambs. However, not all eagle pairs do so and some kill more than others. Overall, predation was found to be relatively low. Between 1999–2002, Mull's nesting eagles consumed an average of 200 lambs each year. From analysis of remains, it was estimated that less than 50 of these were taken alive. In addition, this takes no account of whether those killed were in good enough condition to survive. The report concluded that the presence of sea eagles on Mull is not damaging to sheep farming on a broad scale but that does not preclude localised difficulties in some years.

The issue of living alongside predators goes far beyond economics and mistakes have undoubtedly been made in nurturing a coexistence between this particular predator and human self-interest. Whether conflict between sea eagles and sheep farmers on Mull could have been predicted 30 years ago is a matter of debate but clearly communication and consultation are vital for any future reintroduction of species that are likely to impact on human activities. With further sea eagle reintroductions imminent for central Scotland and eastern England, the management template now operating on Mull can be used to nurture greater understanding of the needs of eagles and people alike.

The following day with the weather easing, the late morning ferry pulls into port. Within minutes the small village of Craignure is a hive of activity. Amongst the melee, Richard Atkinson and David Woodhouse – two local wildlife safari guides – are trying to locate their guests for the day. Richard finds his last couple but before he can leave, a man presents himself as a local hotel owner. "Where can I take my guests to find sea eagles?" he enquires. Richard has become accustomed to this question and remains gracious, suggesting a nearby, easily accessible viewpoint over eagle country.

David Woodhouse of Isle of Mull Wildlife Expeditions is similarly loading baggage into his smart silver transit minibus. With everyone aboard, we join his group and head off down a single track road.

David Woodhouse scans the skies for eagles.

We are quickly reminded of the intensity of eagle protection on the island with signs strategically placed advising that CCTV cameras are in operation in the area. As we round a tight corner, three cars and a minibus block the road, their passengers lined up on a ridge nearby with telescopes and binoculars all pointing the same way and we conclude they must be watching sea eagles.

Our group has arrived on Mull from Wiltshire, Devon, Somerset, France and USA as well as a local couple from the mainland. They are

Golden eagles are also high on a birdwatcher's wish list.

a mixed bunch and include two young children, Zoe and Josh, who look somewhat bemused at the frantic activity.

We thread our way between the cars but have no luck finding eagles further down the road. On our return, the crowd has dispersed. David knows this site looks directly onto a nest – something he's not usually keen to point out but he agrees to a two-minute stop.

Our group climbs the ridge and one lady watcher who has been there for over an hour reports that the male has just brought a lamb to the nest. There is no way of knowing whether it was killed or scavenged but clearly some people are surprised that sea eagles eat lambs. "So they must actually fly along with the lamb?" queries one guest, "I didn't realise they were that strong." For many, this is their first ever sea eagle sighting and they are thrilled. Bill Tucker from Somerset says, "I've never seen a sea eagle before and that's why I'm here – simple!"

Our guide for the day, David Woodhouse has lived on Mull for 20 years and pioneered wildlife tourism on the island. He is passionate about conservation and is campaigning for the area to become Britain's first marine national park. He is also a vehement supporter of eco-tourism – not just wildlife but the philosophy of low impact, sustainable tourism with the benefits being spread throughout rural communities.

He would like to see a much higher standard of service throughout Scotland. He knows the customer demand is there but laments, "There is no strategic thinking on eco-tourism issues. We should be providing visitors with good quality, eco-friendly lodging, feeding them local organic produce and thinking more imaginatively about interpretation – not just about wildlife but about history and geology. Things are improving," he pauses, "but I'm impatient," he says smiling.

The tops of the hills are shrouded in cloud as we drive west towards Loch Scridain. The passing places along the road are dotted with cars

and an array of optical equipment. It seems everyone is looking for eagles. Suddenly, the minibus lurches into a lay-by and David ushers everyone out. Zoe and Josh grab their binoculars and follow David onto a ridge. He's spotted a distant golden eagle, which has now landed on a heathery hillside. Even with a high-powered spotting 'scope, some guests have difficulty picking the eagle out. The bird remains motionless for an hour – as eagles often do – and lunch is declared. Home-made soup and sandwiches followed by delicious scones temper the cold wind. Other cars have joined us now attracted by the activity. "It's like finding a cheetah in the Masai Mara," comments one of our group.

Zoe and Josh are fed and watered and are keeping themselves warm doing eagle impressions on a nearby knoll. They are obviously enjoying the freedom and fresh air even if they can't see the bird.

David's mobile rings – it's his wife Joy. After several minutes of head-scratching and heated discussion, he returns to the group. "I hate turning business away," he says, "but you can only do so much." His tours are full for the next ten days and you might be forgiven for assuming his enthusiasm would dwindle with such a relentless programme. Not on today's evidence. He clears up the lunch dishes and, with the golden eagle still resting, he announces we are going looking for otters. Josh jumps up and down with excitement. "Hooray, otters are my favourite!"

SEEING RED

No other British predator polarises sentiment like the fox. Some go to extreme lengths to rescue and rehabilitate individual animals whilst others routinely wipe out entire fox families. The fox has become the epitome of confused attitudes towards Britain's predators: the ultimate symbol of predator schizophrenia.

It's a balmy summer evening in West Malling, a typical suburban village in a quiet corner of Kent. On the porch of a rambling Victorian rectory, Mike Towler sits smoking a fat cigar. The animal curled up on his lap fast asleep is not a purring cat but a red fox. Cropper the fox once lived in the wild but contracted toxoplasmosis when he was bitten by a dog, leaving him with mental difficulties. Tonight is Cropper's bath night and Mike gently lowers him into the sink before lathering his fur with shampoo. After being rinsed off, he is carried indoors and given a thorough blow dry before the ablutions are completed with a good brushing. Clean and content, Cropper falls asleep on his chair. "All foxes require interaction with other foxes," explains Mike. "Cropper needs interaction with me and he needs to know that I want him." Their relationship is clearly founded on mutual trust.

Cropper is not the only fox that lives with Mike. For more than ten years, he has fed wild foxes and rehabilitated injured or orphaned animals before returning them to the wild. Presently, he has five cubs from the same family, all rescued from the bulldozers at a development site. "I'm fascinated by foxes," he tells us. "Years ago, I realised how organised, how intelligent they are and I set out to find what makes them tick; what it is like to be a fox."

Later, when the cubs are fed, Mike sets out a number of bowls of food on the lawn. It's not long before a young vixen appears. "This is Little Ears," Mike whispers. A few minutes later, a dog fox emerges from the darkness. "And this is Echo." Mike leaves but promptly returns with Cropper around his neck. He calls encouragement to Echo and he immediately responds by taking food from Mike's hand. The interaction

continues through the night and it's four in the morning before Mike
eventually retires.

Clearly captivated by his foxes, Mike is nevertheless aware of popular
misconceptions about this most enigmatic of predators. His wife
Renate runs a bed and breakfast and one day had a family staying
when Mike walked in with Cropper. "The mother instantly grabbed her
child and picked her up in fear of Cropper attacking," Mike recalls. "I
asked the little girl if she wanted to hold Cropper but she replied that
she might get eaten like the gingerbread man."

The residents of West Malling take little notice as Cropper leads Mike
along on his daily walk past the neatly tended houses and gardens. As
we get back home, Mike reflects on our fickle relationship with foxes.

*Mike's neighbour is a poultry farmer and
recently had 30 birds killed which he gave to
Mike to feed to the fox cubs. The culprit in
this case was not a fox but his own dog.*

TOOTH & CLAW

"Of course they can cause problems," he says, "but most difficulties can be avoided if we make a little effort. As the world gets smaller, mankind faces a choice. We can either destroy anything that doesn't suit our way of life or we can learn to live alongside wild animals as respected neighbours. Both sides will make mistakes because we need to learn about each other. But there will be rewards."

"FOXES ARE LIKE PEOPLE. THEY ARE SOCIAL AND FORM MEANINGFUL FRIENDSHIPS BUT THEY SELECT THEIR FRIENDS WITH CARE."

MIKE TOWLER

Foxes are undoubtedly one of our most closely-watched and talked about wild animals. Britain has always been awash with fox stories and there is never a shortage of people willing to tell you, with the voice of authority, that the fox is cruel, ruthless and untrustworthy on the one hand or beautiful, benign and blameless on the other. Everyone has a view and whilst in the past that view might have been influenced by factors far removed from personal experience, the fox's colonisation of our towns and cities within the last generation or so has provided the opportunity for millions to live alongside our largest land predator and decide for themselves whether the wily, dangerous creature portrayed in mythology, paints a true picture.

It is estimated that around 250,000 adult foxes live in Britain, a figure that has been relatively stable for several decades. Each year, a new generation almost trebles that number but by the following spring around 420,000 foxes will have died. Old age, disease, fights with other foxes, traffic accidents and deliberate killing all contribute to such a high level of mortality. But no matter how many foxes die, at a species level they have an incredible ability to survive.

The red fox is the most widespread carnivore in the world and its adaptability ensures that it can survive in almost any habitat from remote mountain forests to our dense urban jungles. Foxes are opportunists. In a rural environment they will scavenge carrion and hunt a wide range of prey from worms to rabbits, whilst research suggests that foxes living their lives in our towns can receive a third of their food from direct human handouts or by scavenging leftovers.

In the absence of larger carnivores, Britain's foxes are largely predator-free. In Scotland, golden eagles can and do take foxes and skirmishes with badgers can sometimes lead to fatal injury but by and large the British fox faces only one main predator: Man. We kill foxes on a massive scale. We snare them, shoot them, dig them out of their earths, hunt them and mow down around 100,000 each year on our busy roads. It is estimated that at any one time, up to a third of adult foxes have healed fractures, many resulting from collisions with cars. But even this heavy toll fails to impact on the overall population, raising questions about the effectiveness of controlling foxes and whether there is any point in expending huge effort in rescuing and rehabilitating individual animals.

Foxes are opportunists and have capitalised on our throwaway lifestyles but the popular myth of them raiding dustbins is rooted in staged photographs like this one.

A fox faces far greater danger from the motor car than it does from the gun.

A golden eagle is powerful enough to bring down a fox but is more likely to feed on one that is already dead.

Andy and Gay Christie run Hessilhead Wildlife Hospital on the outskirts of Glasgow. Back in 1970, their first patient was a fox and since then, demand for their dedicated expertise in treating wild animals has grown significantly. Hessilhead now receives around 3,500 animals a year – from bats to badgers, from swans to seals...and a lot of foxes. "Our foxes are mainly road traffic accidents and young cubs that people find and think they are abandoned," says Gay.

Hessilhead hand-rear their foxes and group them together with similarly-aged animals to try and establish a natural hierarchy. They are then released in early autumn at a time when fox families would naturally disperse.

"To rear and release a group of young foxes probably costs us around £600," Andy tells us. "We feel that each individual matters and that we have a duty to try and rehabilitate these animals, especially bearing in mind that nearly all of the problems we deal with are human-related."

In spite of Glasgow's foxes having integrated themselves into the urban community, it appears that in some cases, familiarity does little to heal our intolerance of nature. Hessilhead was recently contacted by Glasgow's Social Services. "A fox was leaving its droppings on the lawn of an elderly gentleman," Andy tells us. "He wanted the fox 'getting rid of' as the council was refusing to cut his grass on health and safety grounds."

It is easy to understand the motivation for caring for young foxes but once released, this little cub will do well to see his first birthday.

Whilst urban foxes can sometimes cause localised tensions, it seems that most people are delighted that a wild, resourceful animal chooses to live in their midst. Surveys have shown an overwhelmingly positive attitude toward Britain's foxes with many people actively feeding them in the same way they would garden birds. But charity can be short-lived when an opportunistic predator turns its attention on something of value to us. Although relatively rare, foxes do predate pets. Gerbils, guinea pigs and rabbits are all potential targets but contrary to popular myth, cats are quite safe. On farms and smallholdings, ducks and chickens are definitely fair game to a fox.

"TO REAR AND RELEASE A GROUP OF YOUNG FOXES PROBABLY COSTS US AROUND £600."

The killing is one thing but it is often the methodology employed which causes greatest irritation. Given the chance, foxes appear to go into a frenzy of killing that goes far beyond their immediate need for food. This earns them the title of 'wanton killers', a term often used by those who have experienced heavy poultry, gamebird or lamb losses. People who 'dislike' foxes often accuse them of killing just for fun or out of malice but the practice of so-called surplus killing is not confined to foxes. Predators rarely have the luxury of an abundant food supply and often have to make do with what they can get rather than what they need.

Professor David MacDonald is Founder and Director of the Wildlife Conservation Research Unit (WildCRU) at Oxford University and has spent much of his life studying foxes and other wild canids. "It seems that surplus killing is triggered by abnormal behaviour on the part of the prey rather than the predator," he tells us. "In the case of a poultry house or pheasant pen, foxes are confronted by the bizarre situation of prey that doesn't flee. Under these abnormal circumstances, a fox will do what any predator will do – seize the opportunity." Left undisturbed, a fox will usually remove the prey over a period of time, often caching it for later use with little regard for the sell-by date!

What about the accusation that foxes enjoy killing? David continues: "The sensation that we recognise as pleasure presumably evolved as a reward to those individuals that behaved in a way that promoted the survival of the human species – eating and mating for example. Since predators must kill to survive, it is not unreasonable to conclude that they might well enjoy killing, assuming that they are subject to emotions recognisable to humans. I have watched foxes surplus killing and certainly their postures and expressions could support the theory that they enjoy killing. This said, it is nonsensical to judge foxes according to human cultural values."

But of course we do. And we evaluate our management approach to most predators according to our own values. In the case of the fox, economics is hugely influential to how people perceive this animal and how sympathetic they are to various forms of control. It is widely accepted that foxes do impact on livestock farming and game interests and that there is at least some justification in controlling them in areas where such activities predominate. Or is there?

"IT IS NONSENSICAL TO JUDGE FOXES ACCORDING TO HUMAN CULTURAL VALUES."

A great deal of research has been carried out to determine the impact of foxes on the countryside economy. It is estimated that the total cost of fox predation to farmers is £12million annually. Studies have also been carried out to evaluate the cost-effectiveness of controlling foxes on sheep farms measured against the additional costs associated with improved livestock husbandry – indoor lambing for example. The equation is complex and hugely variable on a regional or even local level. Assumptions have to be made about what foxes eat in a given area and therefore their impact on a particular land use, yet their catholic tastes makes this an almost impossible task. Moreover, perceptions rather than science often governs the amount of effort put into fox control.

David MacDonald's research revealed that 46% of farmers surveyed considered they had never lost a lamb to foxes. Overall, the average farmer thought they had lost about two lambs each year to fox predation. Interestingly, very few farmers surveyed reported ever having seen a fox attack a lamb. A more recent survey reported that 59% of farmers said that they had lost at least one lamb to foxes during their most recent lambing. The question of how many healthy lambs are killed by foxes and whether fox control can reduce losses, remains unanswered.

It is estimated that on Scotland's open hill ground, foxes kill about one in every 15–20 lambs that die. However, on places like Mull, where there are no foxes, lamb survival is no better. Other research in upland habitats suggests that no matter how many foxes are killed during the winter, lamb losses the following spring are unaffected and that fox numbers are limited by food availability rather than control by gamekeepers or shepherds. The answer to whether fox control is cost-effective depends on a range of factors but in some areas the economic arguments for blanket control are at the very least, questionable. Of course the influence of foxes in our countryside – positive and negative – reaches far beyond sheep farming and losses in some sectors of the rural economy are outweighed by benefits in others.

Rabbits are considered a major pest to agriculture, yet in some areas rabbits comprise over half of the diet of rural foxes. It has been argued that the consumption of rabbits and the subsequent savings to the farming sector, cancels out any lost revenue resulting from livestock predation.

The difficulty in bringing exact science to the debate over the economic impact of foxes means that management will, for the time being at least, continue to be based on perceptions and tradition. Nowhere does this manifest itself more than in the hotly-contested political arena surrounding fox hunting. The widely publicised debate over the rights and wrongs of hunting foxes with dogs is probably more symbolic of our changing attitudes to predators than any other contemporary issue. So deep-rooted are the entrenched arguments for and against, so heavily charged with prejudice and emotion, that science, even if it were available, would likely be cast aside as irrelevant. Discussions over fox hunting really have very little to do with the fox – the animal has simply become the political pawn in a debate that touches something deeper and embraces conflicting facets of modern society. Rich versus poor; town versus country. The fox has become another symbol in the fight for who should dictate policy for our countryside.

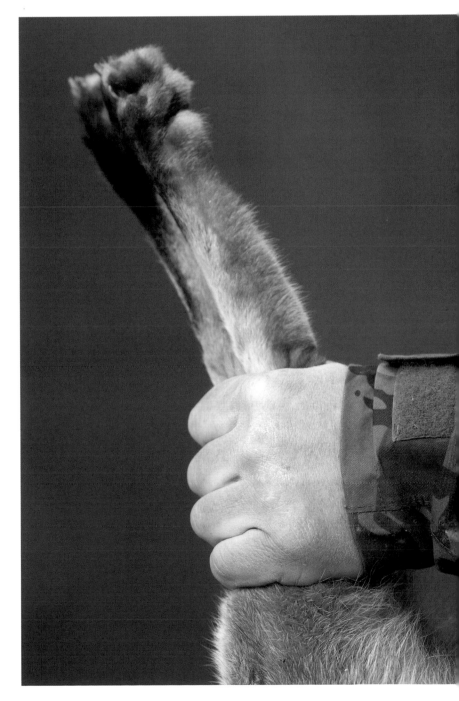

The message is clear and is overtly proclaiming political allegiance but there's no mention of the fox.

The modern form of fox hunting has been practised in Britain for around 250 years. It is said that during the late 19th century a shortage of foxes in England forced hunts to import them from France, Germany and Holland. At the turn of this century, *Baily's Hunting Directory* listed 186 packs of foxhounds in England and Wales and 10 in Scotland. Despite the long tradition, the debate over the hunt's role in modern society has long divided opinion up and down the country.

In 1999, the British government commissioned an inquiry into hunting with dogs. Chaired by Lord Burns, the committee was asked to consider the practical aspects of hunting and its impact on a wide range of rural considerations. In June 2000, Lord Burns submitted to the Secretary of State for the Home Department. 'Without doubt, conducting this enquiry has been a challenging experience. This is a complex issue that is full of paradoxes', he reported.

Hunting foxes with hounds became illegal in Scotland in 2002 and in England and Wales, in 2005. Amidst the celebrations amongst anti-hunting lobbyists, there were widespread claims that in the absence of hunting, foxes would proliferate causing significant increases in economic damage and loss of species diversity. Indeed, following the foot and mouth outbreak of 2001 when fox hunting was temporarily suspended, some sport shooting and farming magazines were reporting a doubling of the fox population.

The suspension of hunting activity brought about through the closure of the countryside also provided researchers with the opportunity to determine the impact of hunting on Britain's fox populations and whether the claims in the countryside press had any credence. The results of a survey published by The Mammal Society in 2002 concluded that the absence of hunting, brought about by the foot and mouth outbreak, had no impact on fox numbers. The subsequent banning of hunting with dogs might have had little ecological effect but the social wounds of the bitter divide continue to fester.

"THIS IS A COMPLEX ISSUE THAT IS FULL OF PARADOXES."

Although only a stone's throw from Leicester with its burgeoning population of 300,000, the sleepy villages around the market town of Melton Mowbray feel as far removed from city life as you can imagine. Reluctant to relinquish the reins of its rural traditions, this country idyll reverberates to the sound of the hunting horn several times each week throughout the winter months.

On a beautifully clear winter's morning, we meet up with the Quorn Hunt which dates back to 1698 and today employs seven staff and keeps 130 hounds. Amidst a sea of horseboxes and four-wheel-drives, the hundred-strong hunt followers gather for a glass of wine before the familiar bugling rallies the hounds. Josh Hambry, Master of the Hunt, bedecked in his bright red jacket and clean white jodhpurs, leads the charge across the Leicestershire countryside.

For the next four hours the progress of the hunt is eagerly followed from every roadside vantage point. The enthralled audience of followers, all avid hunt supporters, have been here many times and some have intimate knowledge of the landscape and the likely hiding places of its resident

foxes. At the end of a long afternoon, we meet up with the huntsmen at a local farm. We've not actually seen a fox but a captive golden eagle has been following the riders all day. Although hunting with hounds is now illegal, the flushing of foxes for them to be killed by shooting or falconers' birds remains legitimate. The eagle has not left the falconer's fist today.

"There is no better way of killing a fox than with a pack of hounds," Josh Hambry enthuses. "Hounds kill the fox instantly, unlike a snare where it has to endure a slow lingering death." The Quorn Hunt has a closed season in spring and summer when the local foxes are breeding. "When they have young I think that they deserve some peace and quiet. It's not nice to think of a vixen being shot and the young starving to death."

Peter Collins has been hunting for 30 years and is in charge of Quorn's hounds. "Hunting has been a part of my family since the time of King Charles," he says. "Without foxes, I'd be out of a job. Besides which, there's a real thrill in the chase and seeing a clean kill – there's no wounding with dogs unlike with shooting."

One of Quorn's most passionate and loyal huntsmen is Robin Smith-Ryland who has ridden with 57 different packs in the UK. "Controlling a pack of hounds is like conducting a symphony orchestra. Many huntsmen hunt to ride but I ride to hunt." Robin spends four or five days each week hunting foxes. "Our main job is fox dispersal, which helps stop them from becoming a problem. In the past when hunting has been suspended, like at the end of the war, foxes were going around in big gangs."

As we leave on a narrow country lane, we pass one of the followers we'd met earlier. He winds down his window. "What we hate is those bloody townies telling us what we can and cannot do."

"MANY HUNTSMEN HUNT TO RIDE BUT I RIDE TO HUNT."

Fox hunting, legal or not, seems to be continuing largely unimpaired by a legislative ruling that many people think is politically driven and unenforceable. Despite nine prosecutions under the Hunting Act to date, there seems little appetite on the part of resource-stretched police forces to prioritise the legislation. The Countryside Alliance consider the legislation to be an attack on what is perceived as the rich and privileged, an issue of class warfare rather than fox welfare. There is also little doubt in the minds of hunt supporters that a repeal in the law is not only imminent but inevitable.

In the meantime, there seems to have been little of the much-publicised impact on traditional rural life but the Countryside Alliance acknowledges that hunting is operating within an atmosphere of compromise which is not sustainable in the longer term.

"WHAT WE HATE IS THOSE BLOODY TOWNIES TELLING US WHAT WE CAN AND CANNOT DO."

Putting the politics of fox hunting aside, the issue of animal cruelty is key to those opposed to hunting with dogs. The fox is a mesopredator, that is to say that whilst it predates some animals, it is also preyed upon by others. With a full complement of native fauna present, fox numbers would be naturally checked by apex predators such as wolves and lynx. Can welfare analogies be drawn between a pack of hounds killing a fox and a natural predator such as a pack of wolves, or a golden eagle? Is there any greater suffering for the fox?

Louise Clark is Communications Officer for the League Against Cruel Sports, one of the principal groups who lobbied for a ban on hunting: "Within nature, animals are either predators or prey, but this is in order to survive and the kill is performed at the first available opportunity. The difference with fox hunting is that the chase is prolonged merely for the sake of human entertainment. This is not a good moral position for a civilised society."

The League maintains that in spite of vociferous opposition to the hunting ban, the majority of the British public favour the Act remaining in place. Only 17% of people interviewed in a post-ban MORI poll wanted to see the Hunting Act repealed.

"Our motivation for lobbying for a ban on hunting was due to the suffering imposed upon wild animals. That foxes suffer unnecessarily was confirmed in the Burns report and is backed up with post-mortem results, which have revealed foxes haemorrhaging and having abdominal wounds that occurred before death," says Louise.

The Burns Report estimated that hunting in Britain before the ban accounted for around 23,000 foxes, or around 5% of the annual number of fox deaths.

"THE DIFFERENCE WITH FOX HUNTING IS THAT THE CHASE IS PROLONGED MERELY FOR THE SAKE OF HUMAN ENTERTAINMENT."

For as long as records exist, foxes have carried the heavy burden of anthropomorphic labelling. We have credited the fox with intelligence and resourcefulness. We perceive it as sly, cunning and crafty. We condemn it for its cruelty and its wastefulness. Misconceptions abound. But the fact is that a fox is just a fox. We may interpret what it does according to a wide range of human values but the fox does not

go out of its way to irritate us, it is simply preoccupied with the difficult business of survival. Its tactics, though not always palatable to our modern perceptions, are no different from those that we have employed ourselves and would do so again should the need arise.

The public pressure that brought about a ban on fox hunting and has driven legal protection for a wide range of other predators would have been unimaginable only a century ago. The charity now extended to the fox by an increasing proportion of the British public is, however, lamented by those who maintain values rooted in rural tradition. Although infinitely resourceful, the fox, like all of our wildlife species, remains largely at our mercy. For the time being, it is enjoying a period of sustained popularity and adapting, even prospering, in a rapidly changing habitat and socio-political climate.

Trends are dangerously fickle however and our relationship with the fox is heavy with contradictions. Although on the face of it the political struggle to outlaw hunting with dogs reflected society's growing sensitivity to animal welfare, it remains entirely legitimate in Britain to shoot a vixen and leave her cubs to a lingering death. The fox population remains ostensibly unaffected by our schizophrenic attitudes and some might say that we can afford to adopt an unregulated, arbitrary approach to its management. However, not so long ago, such a casual approach to all of our predators was deemed to be without consequence.

RUNNING THE GAUNTLET

PIGEONS, PEREGRINES AND PEOPLE

Many of Britain's 60,000 racing pigeon enthusiasts bemoan the recent expansion in peregrine falcon numbers and the impact this has had on their prize birds. Meanwhile, our busy cities with their burgeoning feral pigeon populations are increasingly attracting breeding peregrines much to the delight of urban birdwatchers. The 'hawk problem' is not necessarily a problem for everyone.

It's mid-January and the wind is straight out of the north. The driving rain has a salty taste to it as the surface of the sea is whipped up and over the promenade into the faces of the huddled gathering. The patient queue is a few hundred metres long. At last, a cheer and a round of applause signals the opening of the British Homing World Show at Blackpool's aptly-named Winter Gardens. During the course of the weekend, 25,000 pigeon enthusiasts will pass through the doors where they will scrutinize the 2,500 birds on show and can buy anything from a £30,000 mahogany pigeon loft to a bag of corn feed. An eager crowd surges forward, arms aloft waving soggy tickets.

The hosts, The Royal Pigeon Racing Association (RPRA), promote the event as a family gathering, although the majority of today's show

goers are hardened pigeon fanciers, some donning colourful tattoos, others in smart suits and ties. Things may have moved on from the clichéd attire of cloth caps but the thronging crowds inside the Winter Gardens still share a common bond – a passion for pigeons.

The show is undoubtedly a success and the Winter Gardens is booked to host the event until 2018! By mid-morning, the halls are crammed full with much of the attention directed at the breeding stands. The feel of a bird in the hand holds the secret to its racing potential and this, coupled to a long, stern look into the bird's eye, will determine its saleability. Money changes hands at an alarming rate as fanciers vie to pick up their next winner.

Sometimes life savings rest with the right choice of bird.

Throughout the day, birds from renowned blood lines fetch a few thousand pounds with the big money going on Rosie, a nine-year-old female, who attracts a price tag of £14,000. Many fanciers spend all their spare cash on their birds and more besides.

Although most of the money is still spent on racing pigeons, fanciers are increasingly turning to 'show birds', which can be kept indoors year round. This recent change reflects an increasing frustration amongst racing enthusiasts over the number of their birds being lost to avian predators.

David Hughes is from Colwyn Bay. "We fly our birds from Kent back to North Wales and they are fine until the last ten miles of the journey," he tells us. "The peregrines know where the birds fly and just pick them off. I know fanciers who have lost 50 or 60 birds in a season – the peregrines have annihilated their loft." David is convinced that it's his best birds that are being taken. "The pigeons with brains strike out from the group when they are being attacked – they're an easy target from above. People say it's the weak birds that get taken but it's my star birds that go missing. Some pigeons are worth thousands of pounds, it breaks your heart," he laments.

Peregrines aren't choosy about the price tag on a racing pigeon. They're efficient hunters, taking their prey in mid-flight at speeds up to 200mph.

David admits that some fanciers confront the problem head on. "A few years ago two lads got caught for destroying peregrine eggs and were fined £1,500. We had a whip round for them to pay the fine." David believes that 'problem' raptors should be tranquilised and moved to areas where they do not come into contact with racing pigeons. He blames the RSPB for misrepresenting the number of breeding peregrines. "They would have us believe that there are only 60 pairs in the country but in reality, there are over 150 pairs in Snowdonia alone."

Martin Parry from South Wales paints a similar picture: "I know quite a few lads who have given up racing pigeons altogether. At the end of the day, it's nature but I wouldn't say I was happy about it. There are far too many raptors about and there should be some sort of control just as there was in the war."

Like all fanciers, Dave Holderness from Preston is passionate about his hobby and smiles as he announces that he was the owner of *Home Alone*, which won the World Championship for yearlings back in 1992. He also believes the blame lies at the door of conservation bodies. "These hawks are killing everything. If the birdie groups have their way, there will only be sparrowhawks and peregrines flying around." Dave's club has sent letters to their MP requesting a change in the law that protects raptors but their pleas have thus far fallen on deaf ears. "Don't get me wrong," Dave concludes, "raptors are brilliant birds. I watched a sparrowhawk flying through metal railings to catch a finch – fantastic to watch but they don't do us any good."

There are an estimated 60,000 pigeon fanciers in Britain, represented by five major unions, one of which is the RPRA. Formed over a century ago, it now employs over 30 staff with a turnover in excess of £1million. Pigeon racing has a long tradition in Britain and although historically associated with the working class communities tied to heavy industry, the Royal Family have long been active pigeon fanciers and today maintain lofts at Sandringham in Norfolk. But the hobby is in decline and the RPRA estimates it is losing around 2% of its members each year.

David Power has worked for the North East Homing Union (NEHU) for six years and has been a keen pigeon fancier since he was eight. "I could have owned a mansion if I didn't keep pigeons," he laughs. His voice becomes more serious when we ask about the impact of raptors. "When you drive around, all you see are magpies and hawks – people think raptors are wonderful but it's very distressing to see your pigeon being eaten alive with its heart still beating."

For many, racing pigeons are not just an asset, they're part of the family.

We're invited along to the local working men's club where we meet up with other pigeon racers. The room is full of smoke and the smell of stale beer hangs in the air. Tom Dawson is the NEHU president and owns over 100 racing birds. During the summer months, he is at his loft from five in the morning and his wife Janine cleans out the breeding birds twice a day. On race days, Tom and his friend George will wait by the loft all day to see his birds return. He recalls one

Until relatively recently, peregrine numbers were seriously subdued as persecution, illegal taking of wild birds for falconry and secondary poisoning through organochlorine pesticides, all took their toll. In 1963, numbers were estimated at around 360 pairs. Legal protection has seen numbers bounce back and today, there are around 1,600 breeding pairs in Britain where their main source of prey is wild, feral and domestic pigeons.

A similar, if less spectacular, recovery has occurred with sparrowhawks, which have always been widespread but now number around 34,000 pairs in Britain. It is the larger female which is seen as the greatest threat to racing pigeons and because the prey is consumed whilst still alive, this species is particularly vilified. As regular visitors to garden birdtables, the sparrowhawk often kills its prey in full view of horrified householders and is therefore perceived as a major culprit in the decline of garden birds. It has never been proven however, that sparrowhawk predation limits the breeding populations of their prey species.

The goshawk, a larger, more powerful cousin of the sparrowhawk, was believed to have become extinct in Britain but is now recovering with a population thought to number 450 pairs. Goshawks are presently perceived as less of a threat to racing pigeons but this may change if their range continues to expand.

Goshawks are powerful woodland raptors who prey on crows, grouse and red squirrels. Where pigeons are available, they make a perfect addition to the goshawk's diet.

Although the recovery of these species seems dramatic, their populations are ultimately governed by the availability of prey and suitable habitats in which to nest. Thus, contrary to widespread claims, there is a point at which their populations will stabilise in keeping with natural carrying capacities.

In 1999, following an extensive survey of their 5,200 members in which 90% reported problems with raptors, the Scottish Homing Union (SHU) asked the government to consider a change in the law that would allow pigeon fanciers to protect their stock against raptor attack and to review raptor populations with a view to achieving an acceptable ecological balance with other bird species. Controlling one species in favour of another has historically lead to ecological imbalances throughout the world and in a sensitised Britain, is fraught with ethical and legal complexities.

Presently, racing pigeons are classed as 'domestic' animals and are therefore not afforded protection other than legislation relating to welfare and cruelty. Were racing pigeons to be re-classified as 'livestock', it would be possible for a licence to be granted which would allow the killing of peregrines and sparrowhawks if they posed a serious threat. 'Livestock' however, is presently defined as being for economic benefit or to support livelihoods, making it difficult to prove that racing pigeons merit this status.

A research note produced in response to the petition from the SHU, questioned the level of reported predation, pointed out the legal constraints in affording additional protection to racing pigeons and put forward a conservation view that in order to significantly reduce predation of pigeons, a considerable number of raptors would have to be culled, which would then threaten their conservation status.

To bring some science to the debate, the UK Raptor Working Group commissioned research into predation on domestic pigeons and the results were published in March 2000.

The annual loss of racing pigeons from all causes was found to be 52% and included both old and young birds. Predation by sparrowhawks, goshawks and peregrines varied between each species and according to time of year and geographical region.

Sparrowhawk attacks occur mainly in the vicinity of the loft making them more regularly witnessed by pigeon owners. Although predation rates varied in different areas, the overall impact of sparrowhawks was 3.7% of the total UK racing pigeon population with feral and domestic pigeons accounting for less than 5% of sparrowhawks' diet.

Goshawks, with lower numbers, exerted less of an influence and predation was estimated to represent less than 0.5% of the racing pigeon population. In areas where goshawks have a stronghold however, predation of pigeons can be significant, suggesting that a crossover between hunting territory and racing routes could lead to higher potential losses in the future.

Historically, the conflict between raptors and racing pigeon interests has focused on peregrines. During the 22-week racing season, around 3,800 of Britain's peregrines are presented with 13 million opportunities to take racing birds. One million pigeons will be released into the skies during the first weekend of August alone. Ignoring the east of England where there are few peregrine territories, predation accounted for around 7% of loft losses. Of the racing birds found to have been predated by peregrines, an estimated 70% had either adopted a feral existence or had strayed significantly from their race routes. The remaining 30% were on track to return to their lofts.

The sparrowhawk is much smaller than its close relative the goshawk (left) and it is mainly the larger female that will take pigeons.

The study concluded that straying or the inability to home is the major cause of racing pigeon losses in the UK. From an annual overall toll of 52% of the racing pigeon population, it is estimated that about 7.5% is attributable to raptors.

Pigeons fill the dawn sky at a release site.

There is evidence to suggest that the availability of domestic pigeons in certain areas of the country determines peregrine breeding densities leading to the question of whether large numbers of homing pigeons using a particular flight path actually attract higher numbers of breeding peregrines. Dr Andrew Dixon of Lancaster University suggests that this is the case. "In South Wales, the main population of peregrines feed almost exclusively on racing pigeons. Of course, the highest densities of peregrines occur where there are the greatest densities of pigeon lofts. It makes sense – they have pigeons available all year round. In mid-Wales, there are no race routes and the majority of homers taken there are strays that are already lost."

Could it be then that the presence of racing pigeons if not creating 'the problem' is at least exacerbating any conflict? Is the interest group that is calling for a legalized culling of raptors inadvertently supporting high raptor numbers in some areas? In the same way, should those who feed garden birds be surprised when an opportunistic sparrowhawk seizes the chance for an easy meal? Perhaps 'the problem' is in fact, partially of our own making?

Given the historical urban working-class backdrop to the sport of pigeon racing, it is ironic that in recent years, the peregrine falcon has earned itself celebrity status right in the heart of our busy cities. In 2005, a peregrine pair famously nested at the Tate Modern in central London and attracted over 30,000 visitors in one month amidst the hustle and bustle of the capital. But the London birds are not alone – the British Trust for Ornithology (BTO) estimates that 62 pairs of Britain's expanding peregrine population are now nesting on man-made structures. As vacant territories become fewer, it should not surprise us that new pairs are choosing to settle in urban environments. From a peregrine's perspective, a church tower, an electricity pylon or a high-rise office block is no different to a remote sea cliff. These downtown pieds-à-terre come with fast food on the doorstep...urban pigeons.

Taking full advantage of our modern towns and cities, urban pigeons have proliferated. Where there is a bountiful supply of prey, it's only a matter of time before an enterprising predator moves in.

Edinburgh's pigeon-filled streets provide easy pickings for a city-living peregrine.

The real surprise lies with the unprecedented wave of interest in peregrine watching. These iconic raptors have become members of Britain's charismatic megafauna. They are Exeter's lions, Chichester's humpback whales. They are the fastest animal on the planet and they are coming to a town near you! The combination of urban accessibility and modern technology has brought tens of thousands of people face to face with a wildlife spectacle that, for many, was previously out of reach and perhaps, therefore, irrelevant in their lives. City centre peregrine watching is changing this and delivering a slice of the wild to an enthralled urban audience.

On a bright May morning in Manchester City Centre, Exchange Square is busy. The landscape is dominated by the world's largest *NEXT* store and a huge ferris wheel which breaks the skyline. The trendy boutiques and street-side cafes are enjoying brisk business and above the square, Manchester's Big Screen, which normally showcases United's footballing conquests, is showing grainy black and white footage of four recently-hatched peregrine chicks on a nearby nesting ledge. Incongruously below, local RSPB staff have a telescope trained on one of the city's falcons perched on the balcony of a multi-storey hotel.

"Wow, that's cool," says young Jake Knight as he picks out the bird in the 'scope. Jill Brown, an RSPB volunteer, smiles with satisfaction then collars a passing workman. "Would you like to see a peregrine falcon?" The workman is left with little choice and is almost frog-marched to the telescope. In spite of his reluctance, he seems suitably impressed. "Oh right, I can see it," he says. "Are these the birds I've seen on the telly?" Other passers-by look up at the Big Screen and work out that the telescope must be focused on the real thing. After a

Bradley and Jake – two Manchester lads who think that peregrines are cool.

while, there's a bit of a queue. Jake comes back for another look. He's out for the day with his friend Bradley Mayo and his parents. The boys squeeze themselves to the front and hijack the 'scope. "Bradley's mad on birds," says his mum, "he watches everything on TV that's got anything to do with wildlife. I'd rather that than an obsession with computer games."

After an hour or so, the male peregrine flies off but the interest in the birds continues. Sarah Williams of the RSPB realises how exciting an opportunity this is. "For people to be able to see a bird like this in the middle of Manchester is fantastic," she enthuses. "We've had a few cranky ones who have told us the birds should be shot but most people are thrilled to have peregrines in the city and they follow

There's a sense of pride in having peregrines in Manchester – not every city can boast the world's fastest animal as one of their residents.

their progress almost every day." The local media have dubbed the peregrine soap opera, *Life in Featherfield* and regular updates are featured on TV and radio.

A couple of hours down the M6, there is a similar scene in Derby. This time, the actual nest is on view from Cathedral Green, an open space next to the River Derwent. The Cathedral Peregrine Project goes back to 2004 when one or two birds started using the cathedral tower as a roosting site. The following year, the falcons were seen displaying but in the absence of a suitable nesting ledge, they left at Easter time. In a speculative attempt to encourage breeding, Nick Moyes of Derby Museum installed an artificial platform on the cathedral tower. In 2006, it was occupied and three chicks fledged successfully. Since then, the project – a partnership between Derby Museum, the cathedral and the local wildlife trust – has captured the imagination of not only local people but enthusiasts from all over the world. The web site features live footage of the nesting platform giving unprecedented views of the daily progress of this year's two chicks.

"So far this season, the website has attracted over 60,000 visitors and this is increasing by 3,000 a day," says Nick Moyes. "We're getting comments from all over the UK as well as from USA, Canada and Australia." In addition to the web-cam, peregrine fans can listen to the chicks being fed on *YouTube*, watch the regular news bulletins on TV and sign up for half-term activity days as part of the daily *Peregrine Watch* programme.

"One unexpected angle came when Derby Cathedral's architect was showing other church architects around," Nick tells us. "They all wanted a nesting platform on their churches preferring peregrine pooh on the outside to pigeon mess inside. Derby's church authorities are also delighted with the new audiences they are getting!"

Derby and Manchester are part of an expanding network of cities who can boast nesting peregrines. Up and down the country, these spectacular birds are touching the lives of hundreds of thousands of people – not avid birdwatchers necessarily, just everyday folk going

Nick Moyes will go to extreme lengths to make sure Derby Cathedral's peregrines are doing well.

about their daily lives. Folk who become captivated by *their* peregrines; folk who go on to care a little more about wildlife than they did before; folk who prove that the wild world has a lot to offer us all and that without it, our lives are diminished.

For these people, the prospect of peregrine falcons being culled because of their unwitting choice of prey and their inability to play by our rules, is unthinkable. Predators like peregrines, ospreys and red kites and their willingness to be viewed at close quarters, maintain a tenuous link with the wildness that increasing evidence suggests we all need. For these people, the negative impact of raptors on leisure pursuits is a small price to pay for a wider community benefit and the privilege of living in a world that is still able to support the intricate processes of nature.

BACK FROM THE BRINK

PROTECTING THE PROTECTED

Many of those species taken to the very edge of existence in Britain are clawing their way back following legal protection and, in most cases, improved habitat. Pine martens, buzzards, red kites and even eagle owls are riding the crest of a popularity wave. But already, calls are being heard to limit their spread as they get 'out of control'. When rare predators eat equally rare or valued prey, emotions run high.

The quiet backwater of Dalnavert in the heart of the Cairngorms National Park is hardly the setting for mass murder but last evening, once everyone was safely tucked up in bed, that's exactly what happened. Mike and Dulcie Dixon live in one of nine houses at the bottom of a secluded forest track. They have two children, two cats, one dog and nine chickens. Or at least they did have until last night.

After taking the kids to school this morning, Dulcie went to let the chickens out for the day and noticed that the door to the run was spattered with blood. She fetched Mike and together they discovered the grisly scene – a chicken house littered with the bloodied corpses of nine birds. One had been partially eaten but the others simply bitten and killed. Even Braveheart, their feisty cockerel, had succumbed.

"I understand the cycle of life," sobs Dulcie, clearly distraught, "but I don't understand why they've all been wiped out, it seems so unnecessary." Mike was brought up on Scotland's west coast and is the son of a gamekeeper. "This is a pine marten without question." He's seen such scenes before and is certain of the culprit.

When they return from school, Marsha and Scott are given the news. "I hate pine martens," Marsha cries. Dulcie tries to console her. "You have to accept it," she says, "I don't like it either but everything has a right to live and the pine marten didn't know that they were our chickens."

Just a mile down the road, Balcraggan is a well-tended bed and breakfast and home to Jim and Helen Gillies. The garden is a credit to their hard work and judging by the activity at the bird table, we're not the only ones who appreciate their efforts. Helen makes coffee and hands out delicious home-made cakes. "Years ago, we'd have seen three red squirrels on our bird table whilst we've been sat here," she tells us. "Now we're lucky to see one and that has definitely coincided with more pine martens being around." Helen fetches more cakes. "We hear them on the roof at night and their scats are everywhere – on the lawn, on the patio door – everywhere! A few years ago, we found a den and it had two red squirrel tails in it." Helen thinks that most visitors to this part of the world want to see red squirrels not pine martens. "The powers that be should live-trap the martens and take them to where there are no squirrels," she says.

The Cairngorms is Britain's largest National Park and is home to many rare species. The list is a long one but includes goldeneye, a tree cavity-nesting duck, which although widespread across Scandinavia, breeds nowhere else in Britain. Our native red squirrel has been usurped from most of its natural range by its more adaptable cousin – the introduced grey – but retains its national stronghold in the Cairngorms. And perhaps the most high profile of all is Britain's fastest declining bird and the world's largest grouse, the capercaillie, which holds onto a tenuous existence in the pine forests of northern Scotland. Unfortunately for the pine marten, it has a penchant for all three.

Not so long ago, red squirrels were considered a pest. In 30 years at the turn of the 20th century, the Highland Squirrel Club killed over 80,000. They are now a high-priority conservation species but this doesn't deter a hungry pine marten.

"I DON'T LIKE IT EITHER BUT EVERYTHING HAS A RIGHT TO LIVE AND THE PINE MARTEN DIDN'T KNOW THAT THEY WERE OUR CHICKENS."

Goldeneye nest in man-made boxes – something that pine martens are starting to realise. Wildlife enthusiasts who find their goldeneye predated in their boxes can easily turn against the unwitting predator. Rather than instinctively calling for pine marten control, Allan Bantick places his nesting boxes atop a pole that the marten can't climb. If indeed a problem exists, innovation provides a solution.

Pine martens are a cat-size member of the mustelid family, which includes stoats, badgers and otters. They are found primarily in mature woodland and their core British range is presently restricted to the north-west Highlands. Their diet is surprisingly catholic and includes nuts, berries, insects and small rodents. When they do choose to take larger prey, they're not particularly fussy what it is and certainly take no account of its national rarity. This raises a thorny question: has the pine marten got more or less right to life than the capercaillie or the red squirrel? Who, if anyone, should decide and on what grounds?

Our management of foxes provides an insight into how we might deal with pine marten predation were they common. But they are not common; they too are rare and are protected by the same law that protects their prey species. Although they have undoubtedly expanded in recent decades, fuelling claims that they are 'running out of control', their population is estimated at only around 3,500. Just 3,500. The figure is worthy of repetition as it provides context to the historical abundance of pine martens which were once Britain's second most common carnivore and coexisted with healthy populations of both capercaillie and red squirrels. Records show that during a period of 25 years in the mid-19th century, 427 pine martens were killed on just one West Highland estate. Its recent return, although perceived as dramatic, is incomparable with its former abundance.

As the pine marten reclaims old ground and increasingly comes into contact with human activity, it is stretching some people's tolerance and has prompted calls for its control from both game shooting interests and wildlife enthusiasts concerned about its impact on other species. Others however, recognise the marten's unique ecological role and remain cautious about a knee-jerk reaction which has backfired so many times in the past.

The 'Horse of the Woods'.

Kenny Kortland, Project Officer for the Capercaillie Biodiversity Action Plan (BAP) Group, looks like he's been up all night – probably because he has. It's mid-May and he's just coming to the end of the capercaillie monitoring season, which means his working day starts at 3am. "Many people believe pine martens are limiting capercaillie productivity but the evidence gathered to date does not support this view. In Scotland, capercaillie are doing best in places like Strathspey and Easter Ross and have done so at the same time as pine marten numbers have increased in these areas."

We retire to a local café overlooking the spectacular Cairngorm Mountains. Kenny recognises that the plight of the capercaillie is under public scrutiny not only because it is a flagship species but because of the significant cost involved in its conservation. "It is expensive," he tells us. "Capercaillie need a lot of habitat so we have to do things on a large scale. Grouse biologists that have visited this area from Scandinavia can't believe how we hold onto capers with such small, fragmented pockets of forest. They think it's only possible because we control foxes and crows. They also told me that we need much more forest in order to support robust populations of both predators and prey species. Providing more extensive habitat would reduce the impact of predation."

One of the volunteers involved with capercaillie conservation is Stewart Blair, head gamekeeper on Kinveachy, a traditional sporting estate of 25,000 hectares. He also serves on the committee of the Scottish Gamekeepers Association. He is sensitive to the widely-held negative perceptions of keepers. "It's noticeable that barriers come up when you wear tweeds and introduce yourself as a gamekeeper." He smiles but it's clear that he has given this some thought. "Years ago, keepers used to be God in their own kingdom, many of them unanswerable to their employers. Bad traits got handed down from one generation to the next. It's still like that in some areas but things are changing and I'm a great believer in education in this job – just as in any other."

Stewart doesn't see his job as much different from that of a conservation ranger. "If I took off my tweeds, our profile would be the same – slightly different agendas dictated by our employers but basically we do the same job. I snare foxes to protect red grouse, the RSPB do pretty much the same to protect capercaillie. Communications are strained because of labelling and perceptions – it's not necessary."

Kinveachy is one of Scotland's prime capercaillie estates with extensive tracts of pine forest. Stewart expends considerable time culling foxes but sees no significant problem with pine martens. "Numbers around here are pretty stable and their impact on other species is insignificant."

Stewart Blair: "Things are changing in gamekeeping and I'm a great believer in education in this job."

Whether economics should play a part in measuring the relative worth of a species is hotly contested but financial spin-offs are increasingly being used to justify a particular viewpoint. In the case of pine martens and capercaillie, the books are finely balanced.

Darkness is descending as a tawny owl flies low through the trees and settles in a nearby birch delivering its familiar haunting song. Woodcock are roding overhead and a small herd of red deer emerge to feed on the fresh green grass in a forest clearing. We are on the Rothiemurchus Estate in what can only be described as a deluxe wildlife-watching hide. Our guides, Duncan MacDonald and Malcolm O'Reilly, work for local wildlife tourism operator, Speyside Wildlife. At 9.15pm Duncan asks us all to reduce talking to a whisper – the light is dropping and this feels like a good time for pine martens.

The assembled gathering, all members of the Surrey RSPB Members' Group, are here for a week of wildlife watching and pine marten is top of their list. We wait. A badger emerges from the gloom and eagerly hoovers up the peanuts. He's soon joined by another, then another but no sign of a pine marten. At midnight, we reluctantly leave without a sighting. The mood is sombre. As we reach the end of the forest track with only torchlight showing the way, a marten suddenly appears from the darkness. Everyone stops dead and the moment is electrifying. After a second or two, it disappears over a stone wall and is gone.

"COMMUNICATIONS ARE STRAINED BECAUSE OF LABELLING AND PERCEPTIONS – IT'S NOT NECESSARY."

The following morning with only a few hours sleep, we arrive at the famous RSPB Loch Garten Osprey Centre and at 5am, the car park is already full with vehicles from all over the country. Around 30 people are queuing at the ticket office, all carrying top-of-the-range binoculars and telescopes. None of them have come to see an osprey, they're here for capercaillie. The RSPB open the hide throughout April and early May as there is a good chance of sighting the 'horse of the woods' without the risk of disturbing them in the forest.

Anxious birdwatchers await news of a capercaillie sighting.

By 6am, the hide is bustling with around 80 people eagerly awaiting news of a sighting. The video screen in the corner shows footage from the osprey nest but there is no sign of a caper on TV or in real life. Then, the warden's radio kicks into life: there is a male on show but very distant and very difficult to see. After much jostling for position, we manage to get a look in one of the many telescopes. Sure enough, on a rock on the edge of the forest, a male capercaillie. "Bloody magic," says the owner of the 'scope, "I've driven up from Manchester and for a while I thought it wasn't going to happen."

Concerns over its choice of prey are quickly forgotten when the pine marten is used as an icon for nature-loving tourists.

The Capercaillie Watch attracts around 2,000 visitors in the five-week period it is open. Given the time of day, this is impressive. Equally, Speyside Wildlife's pine marten hide is booked every night even in the winter. Both species are clearly tourism celebrities and bring financial benefits to a wide range of local businesses.

So which one is more worthy of protection? Various pieces of research have been carried out in an attempt to address this question, at least from an ecological viewpoint. Studies into the impact of pine martens on capercaillie have been largely inconclusive with predation certainly taking place but not to a degree where capercaillie populations are adversely affected. In a statement made by the Capercaillie BAP Steering Group in 2005, it was suggested that pine martens are far less important predators of capercaillie than foxes. Given the lack of clear evidence that martens have a detrimental effect on overall capercaillie populations, the Group recommended ongoing research but advised against the control of martens.

For studies into predator-prey dynamics to be representative, it must be assumed that both predator and prey are at 'natural' levels in the study area. In the case of pine martens and red squirrels, few such areas exist in Britain. Nevertheless, prompted by anecdotal evidence suggesting that expanding marten populations were causing reductions in red squirrel numbers, some research has been carried out.

From six studies in Scotland, it has been found that red squirrels are an insignificant prey item for pine martens. This compares starkly with research carried out in Scandinavia where squirrels can form more than 50% of a pine marten's diet. It is clear then that the pine marten – and a number of other predators – have the potential to take large numbers of squirrels where they are available. The question that is not answered is whether we should intervene should this ever become the case?

Maturing forest habitats have helped pine martens expand in recent decades, benefiting a wide range of other species. Including us.

Dave Anderson tracking down a radio-collared pine marten to a tawny owl box.

Mist hanging over the treetops and the vibrant colours of a rain-soaked understorey give an otherworldly feel to the silent forest. On a remote gravelled track, we meet Dave Anderson, Head of Conservation for Cowal and Trossachs Forestry District, an area covering some 70,000 hectares in central Scotland. Dave has worked for the Forestry Commission for 27 years – plenty of time to learn about the forest and its rhythms of life. He has stalked deer and has shot a bear in Canada but his real passion is raptors. With a ringing licence, Dave has worked with all of Scotland's charismatic species and his steely blue eyes reveal a man who cares deeply about wildlife. Dave is no supporter of sentiment however, his approach is a hard-edged hunger for knowledge – undimmed after all his time in the forest.

For 20 years, Dave has been involved in a study on tawny owls nesting in artificial boxes. For much of this time, red squirrels have been a conservation priority in the forest and regularly occupy the tawny boxes. Many of Dave's colleagues feared that once pine martens found their way back, the tawny owl and red squirrel populations would plummet. Now pine martens are back and this year alone, five egg clutches plus one brood of tawny chicks have been predated by martens. Significantly, red squirrels no longer use the boxes.

"I have no agenda with martens," says Dave. "It's great to see them back in this area – they are a natural part of the forest ecology. That is not to say I don't feel hacked off when I discover an empty owl box with egg fragments lying around." Dave is convinced that martens have learnt to associate the nest boxes with food and are systematically targeting them. "In a way, this is our own doing and we must look to make them less vulnerable. This is not because we don't want martens but in providing boxes for tawnies and squirrels, we're effectively providing the local martens with an easy meal."

"IN PROVIDING BOXES FOR TAWNIES AND SQUIRRELS, WE'RE EFFECTIVELY PROVIDING THE LOCAL MARTENS WITH AN EASY MEAL."

Dave is visibly excited about this new dynamic in the forest. "The science of predator-prey relationships fascinates me," he says. "I'm intrigued about the marten's role in the forest."

In another part of Dave's district, there has been a similar ongoing study of barn owls. Through forest restructuring and the installation of nest boxes, barn owl numbers have risen from three to forty pairs in 15 years.

When the barn owl boxes were first put up, there were no pine martens but a sizeable population of grey squirrels, many of which used the boxes. Pine martens are now present in force and of 180 boxes, none is now occupied by grey squirrels. This region is of particular conservation significance in that both red and grey squirrels are present. Intriguingly, since the pine martens arrived, there are far less greys and the number of reds has increased.

Dave is anxious to point out that this is not science and the survey needs more research but his early perceptions lend an interesting ecological perspective to the plight of red squirrels in areas where they are under pressure from greys. Is the pine marten in fact a potential ally to the native red squirrel?

Dave intends to radio-collar more pine martens to establish their movements more effectively but is in no doubt about what the longer term plan should be. "Ultimately, we need more robust habitats supporting populations of all species, which can withstand the pressure of predation."

Johnny Birks of the Vincent Wildlife Trust has over 20 years experience of pine marten research and co-ordinates new sightings to establish whether martens are expanding in England. "There is a steady trickle of convincing records," says Johnny, "and we can conclude that pine martens are slightly more widespread in England and Wales than ten to twenty years ago." Johnny is not convinced however, that the marten can establish itself in a meaningful way beyond its present range. "In Europe, martens do best in ancient woodland where there are lots of natural den sites. In Scotland, they'll use craggy, rocky areas but neither habitat is widespread beyond the highland fringe."

Johnny is also aware of anti-marten sentiment and is frustrated at our apparent inability to find imaginative ways of dealing with any conflict. "Rather than reaching for the trap and gun we need to look for more sustainable ways to allow coexistence."

The future for Britain's pine martens seems uncertain. "Our present 10–15% woodland cover is not enough," says Johnny. "We need 30–40% and it will be 150 years before trees are large enough to provide den sites. Some people may perceive that pine martens are out of control but in reality they are hanging on in sub-optimal habitat."

There are millions of people who feed their garden birds but not many can claim to attract hundreds of large raptors to their bird table...all at the same time! Chris Powell owns Gigrin Farm, near Rhayader in central Wales and is known locally as 'The Kite Man'.

Fifteen years ago, Gigrin was a typical Welsh sheep farm that just happened to be right in the middle of Britain's only remnant population of red kites. Persecuted to extinction in England and Scotland, red kites got caught up in the systematic onslaught of Britain's raptors and were reduced to just a handful of breeding pairs in the remote ancient oakwoods of the Welsh valleys. Chris recalls a winter roost of just six kites on the farm back in the early 90s. "The birds were always interested in rabbit remains around the fields," Chris recalls, "so one day my father cut one up and threw out the pieces – whoosh – the kites came straight in, we couldn't believe it."

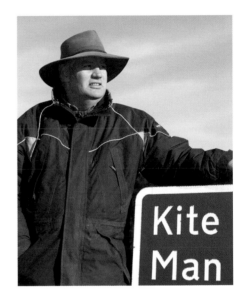

The RSPB, conscious of the precarious status of Wales' last kites, asked Chris' father, Eithel, if he would help in establishing an official feeding station. "We had an interest in wildlife," says Chris, "so we fed the kites every day at 2pm and in 1992 we had twelve birds visiting regularly."

The story since then is a remarkable one. Gigrin Farm now has five large viewing hides with plans for another two and attracts up to 400 kites, a dozen or so buzzards and numerous ravens at peak times of the year. "It's fantastic," Chris enthuses, "but my meat bill has gone up to over £1,000 per month!"

Gigrin accommodates 36,000 visitors a year and has become part of 'Kite Country', a local marketing initiative which gives this picturesque corner of Wales a real identity on the tourism map.

On the day of our visit, there is a couple who have driven six hours from Newcastle just to see the kites for the day. There is a young family from Shropshire who are enthralled by the spectacle:

"We've never seen anything like it, it's just amazing." Chris has grown used to the reaction of visitors. "The support from the public has been tremendous. We've had visitors from Scotland and the Isle of Wight just for the afternoon – you'd be staggered what people do."

Sadly, Chris' father died in 2005 but the business that Eithel started continues to flourish. It is obvious that Chris has a genuine respect for these magnificent birds and still enjoys the spectacle of feeding time. "You can't relate the experience to people," he says, "you've got to come and see it for yourself."

"WE'VE NEVER SEEN ANYTHING LIKE IT, IT'S JUST AMAZING."

In an attempt to reinstate red kite populations elsewhere in Britain, a series of reintroductions was initiated in 1989 with birds being restored to northern Scotland and the Chilterns from surplus chicks in Sweden and Spain. Since then, further reintroductions have taken place in

Northamptonshire, Yorkshire, Dumfries & Galloway and Tyne & Wear. There are now an estimated 800 pairs breeding in Britain.

Although the red kite is one of the UK's largest birds of prey, it is primarily an opportunistic scavenger and lacks the strength and power needed to kill anything larger than a small rabbit. Knowledge of its feeding biology however, has not been enough to gain it a universal welcome. One tale of an old lady in Northampton who, on seeing a kite circling overhead, scooped up her Yorkshire terrier and fled to the sanctuary of a nearby butcher's shop, belies a more serious resistance to the return of predators to our countryside.

In 2006, the RSPB claimed that almost half of Scotland's kites were believed to have been illegally killed as a result of eating poisoned carcasses left out for corvids and other raptors. Although rarely the intended victim, the kites' tendency to scavenge makes them highly susceptible to poisoned meat. It is noteworthy that the Chilterns in England and the Black Isle in northern Scotland were the two original sites for red kite restoration in 1989. In 2005, 250 pairs of kites successfully bred in the Chilterns whilst there were only 39 nesting pairs on the Black Isle, although both habitats are comparable.

Buzzards have always retained a stronghold in the West Country but are now spreading throughout Britain.

A red kite fledgling is weighed and tagged for future monitoring.

Our knowledge of predator biology and advances in technology have afforded us the ability to not only restore previously diminished predator populations but to manipulate other species to our own ends. But achieving agreement on how, or whether, we should exercise that ability and which species should be prioritised, is tricky and controversial. And the next dilemma is always just around the corner.

The eagle owl is Europe's largest owl, is ten times heavier than a long-eared owl and can kill other large birds of prey, foxes and even domestic cats. In spite of reports of isolated breeding in the UK, the eagle owl has generally always been accepted as a non-native species with those few present believed to have originated from illegal reintroductions or birds that have escaped from private collections. In 2005, a BBC TV documentary revealed that a pair of eagle owls had been breeding on MOD land in North Yorkshire for nine years and had produced 23 young during this time. The debate over whether the eagle owl should be declared as a natural coloniser and afforded full legal protection or whether it should be removed as a non-native threat to other rare species, immediately hit the headlines.

Julian Hughes is RSPB's Head of Species Conservation. "How we think about eagle owls depends on whether they are native to Britain or not. If they are, or they prove able to get here from Europe under their own steam, the RSPB welcomes them back as part of our natural heritage. If they are not, it illustrates how islands have their own unique wildlife, separate from mainland Europe."

"At the moment, there is little evidence that the eagle owl has occurred naturally in the UK in recent centuries, and most experts agree that the small breeding population originates from captive birds. Their removal may be justified if they are not native and likely to have a negative impact on native species, whether as prey or competitors," he says. "The dilemma is whether we should wait until any impact is serious, by which time removing them could be a great deal more difficult."

"HOW WE THINK ABOUT EAGLE OWLS DEPENDS ON WHETHER THEY ARE NATIVE TO BRITAIN OR NOT."

Recent research in Switzerland has revealed the species' ability to fly over long distances and although it is not yet known whether the owls will cross open sea, the expanding population of Europe's eagle owls might support the theory that birds now breeding in Britain may in fact be an overspill from the European mainland.

Tony Warburton of The World Owl Trust suggests that the caution expressed towards eagle owls has more to do with its size and expertise as a predator than science, logic or fact. "We believe the British Ornithologists Union should now add eagle owls to the official list of British birds and that the species should receive the same protection as any other bird of prey."

The opportunity for the Yorkshire eagle owls to provide some of the answers to a growing list of questions has, for the time being, been denied. A month after the documentary was shown, the female was shot and later died from her wounds. Tony Crease works for the MOD as Deputy Commander of Defence Training Estate (North) based in Catterick and has been monitoring the owls since they first arrived. "Many people knew about the owls so I'm sure the TV exposure made no difference," he says, "but the bird was found with BB shot in it – commonly used by gamekeepers to shoot foxes."

Tony finds it difficult to understand why eagle owls might be perceived as a problem. "I've made around 70 visits to the nest over the years and prey remains were almost entirely rabbits. We have black grouse, kestrels and buzzards here but I've never seen the eagle owls bother with them. Equally, if they were killing lambs, the farmer wouldn't put up with it."

Since the female was killed, two other eagle owls have been seen in the area but there is no way of knowing if they're breeding or where they came from. Around once a fortnight, Tony receives photos of eagle owls from all over the country. "I've been sent plenty of photos taken on North Sea oil platforms," he says, "these birds are flying over from Europe, there's no doubt about that."

Tony believes that eagle owls are far more numerous than we think. "They're bloody difficult to see," he says, "and they'll never reach plague proportions. These so-called experts who are peddling nonsense about eagle owls decimating bird populations should know better."

"HAVE YOU HEARD ABOUT THOSE EAGLE OWLS IN YORKSHIRE. I'VE BEEN TOLD THAT THEY'LL BE AS COMMON AS BUZZARDS SOON."
MEMBER OF THE QUORN HUNT, LEICESTERSHIRE

The potential establishment of the eagle owl in Britain will undoubtedly test our tolerance, prejudices and inconsistencies as have many of the predators who have recently returned from the brink. We deem that we have a duty to make value-judgements on the impact of predators on their prey species and to assess the relative contributions that individual species make to our ecosystems.

It may be however, that we are entering a period where some predator species are returning to the levels at which they would have been found before we exerted such a strong influence, and that we are simply not accustomed to allowing nature a free rein. Perhaps we've never had the ability to stand by and allow predator-prey dynamics to flourish. Perhaps we never will.

LIVING
ROOM LIONS

THE PAMPERED AND
THE FORGOTTEN

As a nation we seem to be obsessed by cats – around nine million share our homes as pets. The impact of this many predators on our garden birds and mammals causes widespread resentment but meanwhile, the wild cousin of the domestic cat is perilously close to extinction and very few seem to care.

There are screams of excitement coming from all over the house as the Dudgeon girls play hide and seek with their new companions. Their mum Lesley rolls her eyes in despair but a soft smile reveals her secret affection for the new additions to the family. Occasionally, one of the bright-eyed young kittens dashes across the living room floor and takes temporary sanctuary under the sofa. There are six bundles of fur and energy somewhere in the house along with their mother Belle, who has retired to the solitude of the utility room. "The kittens are great for the kids," says Lesley Dudgeon. "They play with them for hours and it will break their hearts when they have to go." All six kittens are promised to local homes. Some of these already have a cat but the temptation to take on another is just too much. It's easy to see why.

This is Belle's second litter in six months. She spends most of her time prowling the local woods and Lesley has no idea how far she ranges or who the father of the latest kittens might be. "She comes back when she's ready!" Nine-year-old Catriona comes in holding three of the kittens. "If you want a photograph, you'll have to be quick," she tells us. Sure enough, within seconds, the kittens are away, scampering off in different directions.

It is clear that both Catriona and her sister Fiona are smitten with their cats and they're not alone. Around a quarter of British households own a cat and for many children, this early contact with an animal builds the foundation for a wider affinity and respect for other species. Cat ownership or 'care-giving' as American cat lovers prefer it to be known, is on the increase but for some, having a cat around the house reaches far beyond simple companionship.

It's a blustery day as we meet up with Anne Haddow at her remote croft on Skye's west coast. It is fair to say that Anne is a cat fanatic. "They are my family," she says earnestly. "These cats really are my children and I'd protect them with my life." At one time, Anne had 28 cats but over the years, this has reduced to four. Anne's croft was partially destroyed in the hurricane that swept across the Hebrides two years ago, so she now lives seven miles away and cycles to feed her cats every couple of days. "Every cat should be allowed to have kittens," she says. "At least one litter." Anne disagrees with the popular view that free-ranging cats should be neutered.

The issue of cat predation on birds and small mammals is a sensitive one so we broach the subject with caution. "My cats don't go for that many birds, they mainly catch voles," Anne asserts. "If cats are well fed, they don't really bother wildlife – they may take the odd bird but they don't wipe out populations as some people claim."

Dr Rima Morrell of Living Ark, an animal sanctuary nearby, agrees. "Cats do not have an uncontrollable desire to hunt," she says with authority. "They are more likely to hunt when they're unhappy about something – it's often a sign of disapproval." Dr Morrell works in the field of human-animal therapeutics and is convinced that cats have an emotional capacity. "When I first started seeing my future husband, one of my cats was obviously jealous of him and regularly left dead mice on the pillow of our bed in protest."

Catriona Dudgeon and friends.

"EVERY CAT SHOULD BE ALLOWED TO HAVE KITTENS – AT LEAST ONE LITTER."

In addition to providing a rescue and re-homing service, Living Ark stages educational events which explore the medical and spiritual benefits of companion animals. Dr Morrell: "Cats make ideal pets and it is clinically proven that stroking a pet reduces blood pressure and has healing properties."

The claim that a close association with a pet can enhance our psychological well-being is widely held. Studies by Pets as Therapy (PAT), a charity dedicated to improving the lives of nursing home residents and those in recovery centres, shows that even brief contact with a dog or a cat can significantly improve mood states.

Kate Jack and Charlie – regular visitors to local hospitals and day care centres where Charlie has become something of a celebrity.

Kate Jack is a PAT volunteer and regularly visits hospitals with Charlie, her pet rescue cat. "Pets break down barriers and help interaction with people, especially those with conditions like dementia," she tells us. "Many people have a pet at home so PAT pets fill a void and gives them something to cuddle." Kate sees huge benefits in people having close contact with animals. "I recently visited someone who had been housebound for years and had become depressed. When a PAT cat visited and stayed, their depression lifted and they were able to laugh for the first time in years."

It is estimated that Britain's cat population exceeds nine million – twice what it was 30 years ago. Clearly cats give their owners a great deal of pleasure, comfort and, in some cases, emotional support. For some, children especially, a pet compensates for an increasing lack of contact with nature that came as a standard part of childhood even a generation ago. For elderly people, now living longer than ever before, a pet cat provides invaluable companionship in later life.

The biological perspective that questions the moral responsibility for effectively releasing this number of non-native predators into the environment, is therefore highly emotive and hotly contested. Cats are instinctive hunters but for many owners, a few dead birds or mice courteously delivered to the back door, is an acceptable consequence of living with an efficient predator. Not everyone agrees.

"IT IS PART OF NATURE FOR CATS TO HUNT. NOTHING WRONG WITH THAT. MY CATS OFTEN BRING ME 'PRESENTS'. SOMETIMES ONLY THE HEAD!"
TOOTH & CLAW CONTRIBUTOR

Research commissioned by The Mammal Society suggests that between them, our pet cats catch 275 million individual prey items each year. Fifty-five million of these are birds with the most frequent victims being house sparrows, blue tits, blackbirds and starlings. If these figures are correct, such a heavy toll on our native wildlife would make the domestic cat by far and away our most prolific predator.

A wolf in sheep's clothing?

Such statistics cultivate strong anti-cat sentiment across a broad range of interest groups and individuals. Over recent years, calls have been heard for control measures ranging from compulsory cat licensing and/or neutering, curbing the freedom of cats to roam at will and the requirement that all cats wear bells to mitigate their hunting success. Cat culling is also a frequently-voiced suggestion.

"IF SOMEONE'S DOG CAME INTO OUR GARDENS KILLING THE WILDLIFE WE'D BE UP IN ARMS. WHAT MAKES CAT OWNERS THINK THEIR PET IS EXEMPT FROM THIS?"

TOOTH & CLAW CONTRIBUTOR

Such resentment is understandable given the emotive issues involved. However, on a scientific level, there is little evidence that cat predation is having an impact on the overall populations of their prey species. Research by The Mammals Society acknowledges that by virtue of their abundance, domestic and feral cats (an estimated 800,000 cats live in a 'wild' state in Britain) are a major predator of wild animals. This is tempered by the considerable variation in the range and number of prey species taken and the inclination of individual cats to capture wild prey. Although the figures are undoubtedly alarming, researchers point out that they should not be used as an assessment of the impact of cats on wildlife populations.

Studies carried out by the RSPB concur with this: 'Despite the large numbers of birds killed, there is no scientific evidence that predation by cats in gardens is having any impact on bird populations UK-wide'. The Society uses the example of blue tits, the second most frequently cat-killed bird, which has increased by over 25% in the last 40 years. Interestingly, several authors have suggested that feeding garden birds may in fact reduce their susceptibility to cat predation. A larger number of birds may be more effective at warning against predator presence and the extra food supply may help reduce foraging time and thus the time the birds are at risk of being captured by cats.

Current studies in urban Sheffield underline the difficulty in drawing definitive conclusions from regional surveys. Victoria Sims, a research student, has been monitoring an area containing 3,000 terraced houses with a cat density of over 1,000 per square kilometre. The majority of cats in this study area are killing on average less than one prey item per year, which suggests the overall toll on wildlife may not be as severe as previously suggested. Approximately 80% of the cats in the Sheffield study didn't catch a single prey item in two and a half years.

"I don't think that urban cats are having as large an impact on the populations of birds and mammals as people imagine," says Victoria. "There is certainly evidence to suggest that predation by urban cats is minimal. That said, undoubtedly some cats have a significant impact at a local level but this is not necessarily a widespread problem."

Interestingly, 60% of cats in Victoria's study area wore collars with bells, a simple yet proven technique for reducing wildlife predation. The RSPB reports that a cat bell can curb the impact of predation by around a third. Separate research studies carried out in Carnforth in Lancashire resulted in a 50% reduction in hunting success for those cats wearing a bell. It should be noted however, that another study revealed that bell-wearing cats become a more stealthy and effective hunter, learning to move so slowly that the bell made no sound!

Predatory species like foxes and crows are routinely and legitimately controlled throughout rural Britain. Those concerned about garden wildlife might argue that reasonable measures should be taken to control the impact of this predator.

"I CONVINCED MY NEIGHBOUR TO FIT LOUD FALCONRY BELLS TO HER CATS AND THE BIRD POPULATION IN OUR GARDEN HAS BENEFITED."

TOOTH & CLAW CONTRIBUTOR

Our inclination to own and care for cats seems to know no bounds. Designer hats, jackets and fluffy bootees are now available for the fashion-conscious feline with selective breeds being touted as fashion accessories. Such lavish affection for our pet cats brings into sharp focus one of the most bizarre inconsistencies of our relationship with all of Britain's predators. At a time when the cat plays a more prominent role in our lives than ever before, its native wild cousin, the European wildcat, faces imminent extinction in Britain. Does anybody care?

Following the last Ice Age, the land bridge connecting us with mainland Europe became the English Channel and two feline species that had made their way north into Britain's forest wilderness became isolated. One, the Eurasian lynx, has long been extinct. The other, the European wildcat, still clings to a tenuous existence in remote parts of northern Scotland. Persecution and habitat loss has driven the wildcat this far north: the animal has been absent from England and Wales since the late 1800s. The Scottish population was significantly eroded with the advent of the sporting estate and the Victorian's lust for spectacular museum specimens. By 1914, the species was almost extinct but a last-minute reprieve came when 20,000 gamekeepers were called to serve in the First World War, many of them never to return.

Over time, the European wildcat evolved both physically and behaviourally and is now regarded as a separate sub-species, the Scottish wildcat. This is an animal that superficially passes as a heavyweight tabby but any resemblance to the cat in your living room ends there. Comparing a true wildcat with its domestic relative is akin to likening a wolf with a labrador. The wildcat is a robust looking animal, its wide head and jaw complementing the distinctive blunt, ringed tail to give the animal a discernible wild demeanour. The wildcat is considered untameable even when captive-reared.

Although the wildcat has made a steady recovery, it presently faces a far more serious and insidious threat than that of persecution, ironically attributable to our love affair with domestic cats.

Scottish wildcat.

This may be one of only 400 left in the wild.

Experts believe that the Scottish wildcat population could be as low as 400, their genetic integrity slowly being diluted by feral domestic cats – the two species will readily interbreed and produce fertile offspring, or hybrids. Given the extreme rarity of wildcats and the abundance of ferals – an estimated 100,000 in Scotland – the likelihood of a meeting between two pure-breds is extremely thin, exacerbating the problem further. Left unchecked, the wildcat gene pool will likely become so influenced by domestic cat genes, the species will die out.

For such a charismatic predator, so enmeshed with Scotland's cultural history, it is difficult to imagine how the wildcat has come to face such a challenging future. In spite of huge resources poured into conserving other high-profile native species, the Scottish wildcat and its potential demise has been largely ignored. Is it too late for the forgotten cat?

Colin Galbraith is Director of Scientific and Advisory Services for Scottish Natural Heritage (SNH): "Very few people have ever seen a wildcat so they just don't relate to them," Colin tells us. "In the absence of any organisation willing to champion its cause, the wildcat has just slipped off the radar."

Just recently, SNH has recognised the severity of the problem, prompted by increasingly loud alarm calls from leading scientists. "Morally, it is not right that we just let it slip away," continues Colin, "and legally we are under obligation to protect the wildcat." SNH has recently prioritised the Scottish wildcat within the Species Framework Directive and commissioned a population study to establish the species' current distribution. Adrian Davis is a consultant ecologist and environmental scientist and is the man faced with that difficult and labour-intensive task.

"IN THE ABSENCE OF ANY ORGANISATION WILLING TO CHAMPION ITS CAUSE, THE WILDCAT HAS JUST SLIPPED OFF THE RADAR."

"Scottish wildcats are now one of Britain's rarest mammals and one of the main threats to their continued existence as a distinct species is their inter-breeding with feral domestic cats," says Adrian.

Due to their secretive nature and the wild areas they inhabit, clear sightings of wildcats are rare. The difficulty in reliably separating sightings of true wildcats with those of feral hybrids, compounds the task. "The last survey of Scottish wildcats took place over 20 years ago," says Adrian, "and to establish accurate figures for this survey we are relying heavily on the help and co-operation of a large number of people where wildcats might be found. If we can establish, within certain limits, a population estimate and distribution map, this will allow conservation measures to be effectively targeted."

With Adrian's survey work underway, Colin Galbraith is upbeat about the wildcat's future. "I feel we have now turned the corner." His optimism is not shared in other areas of wildcat conservation.

People can live their whole lives in wildcat country without ever seeing one. Adrian Davis has to work out how many live in the whole of Scotland.

Allan Paul is a softly spoken native of Elgin in north-east Scotland. He and his wife Morag have a passion for cats. In 2000, Allan was encouraged to resurrect the Scottish wildcat captive-breeding studbook, which records all wildcats in captivity and their suitability for breeding. "The studbook hadn't been updated for a few years," Allan tells us. "None of the zoos or collections seemed to know what they were doing and, more worryingly, some just didn't care." In addition to maintaining the studbook, Allan has five cats in captivity – three hybrids and two pure-bred wildcats. "The long-term plan of the breeding programme is to augment the wild stock through releases but before we can even start thinking about that, the aim is to establish ten pure-bred breeding pairs. Presently, there are only nine individuals considered suitable for breeding in the whole of the UK."

Allan Paul: "We must staunch the flow of domestic cat genes into the wildcat population. Education and increased neutering are essential."

Allan believes that without an extensive captive breeding and release programme, the wildcat will be extinct within a decade. "It's very difficult to be optimistic," he says. "It takes the zoological community so long getting around to doing anything. I'm afraid it's only a matter of time before there are none left."

Allan and Morag have recently decided to give up caring for wildcats and running the country's only studbook. After almost a decade, they have become disillusioned at the lack of support and political will to address the plight of one of Scotland's most emblematic species. At the time of writing, nobody is willing to take on the running of the stud book.

There are detractors of the Scottish wildcat, those who question whether the species in its pure-bred form still exists. Critics of wildcat conservation efforts point out that domestic cats first arrived in Britain some 2,000 years ago – more than enough time to hybridise with their wild counterpart. Allan Paul acknowledges that this perception has had a negative impact on the captive breeding programme and that some zoos and collections see little point in trying to save the wildcat as hybridisation has already gone too far.

A loophole in the law which allows the legal shooting of feral cats, protects those intent on persecuting wildcats, claiming it is impossible to tell the difference between the two.

"I'M AFRAID IT'S ONLY A MATTER OF TIME BEFORE THERE ARE NONE LEFT."

Steve Piper of the recently-formed Scottish Wildcat Association, a charity dedicated to conserving our native feline: "Solving the hybridisation threat is our most important challenge and tantalisingly achievable. The wildcat and its hopes for conservation need some positive PR."

Steve is a committed observer of any scientific developments that may improve wildcat conservation efforts. "Wildcat genes are stronger than domestic genes and Allan Paul's work with his captive wildcats proved that the domestic influence can be selectively bred out," says Steve. The prospects for reliably identifying genetically-pure wildcats has recently been improved with the discovery of the 'domestic cat gene', allowing blood to be tested for any amount of domestic influence.

Dr Andrew Kitchener, Curator at the National Museums of Scotland, is a devotee of the Scottish wildcat and has researched the controversial issue of identification, a reliable and practical method of which is required to effectively implement legal protection and conservation. Past studies have

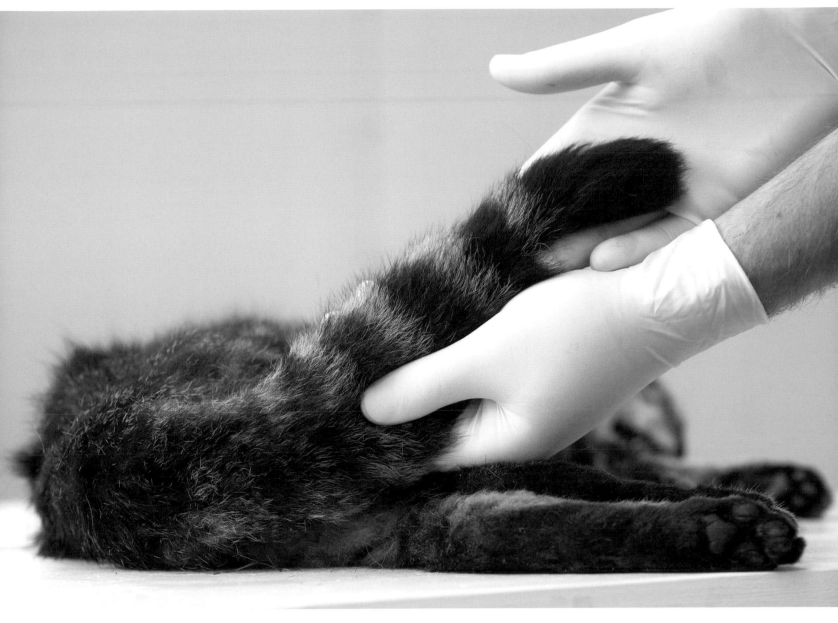

Extensive examination of dead wild-living cats, enables scientists to evaluate their genetic purity.

established morphological characteristics that identify pure-bred wildcats, including cranial and intestinal differences, from feral domestic cats. However, this required a post-mortem examination of a dead animal. To identify and protect live wildcats, a visual diagnosis was needed. By using a number of specimens from museum collections, acquired over an extended time period (100+ years), along with European wildcats showing various degrees of hybridisation, Dr Kitchener was able to establish a set of key pelage characters, which distinguish wildcats from domestic cats and their hybrids. Although ongoing research is required, the seven key criteria identified by

Kitchener allows the possibility to visually identify a true Scottish wildcat in the field for the first time.

The very existence of the wildcat, its present conservation status and its ongoing protection and expansion is scientifically and logistically complex. When compared to the resources channelled into the preservation of the red squirrel, water vole and capercaillie, along with the restoration of the osprey, red kite and sea eagle, the situation facing the Scottish wildcat is, to say the least, bemusing.

Our past treatment of the wildcat is no different from that meted out to all of our predators – it is a familiar and lamentable story, yet excusable given the motivations of the time and the limitations of ecological knowledge. But today, in the conservation-minded 21st century, the wildcat faces the very real threat of extinction and, notwithstanding recent initiatives, remains a low-profile conservation priority in a country of cat lovers.

"THEY'LL FIGHT TO THE DEATH FOR THEIR FREEDOM; THEY EPITOMISE WHAT IT TAKES TO BE TRULY FREE."

MIKE TOMKIES, WILDERNESS AUTHOR

Wildcat country.

MARINE WOLVES

Everyone wants a slice of what lives in our rivers and oceans and at a time when fish stocks are critically low and legislation is curbing further exploitation, it is easy to point the finger at other predators that compete with us for nature's bounty. Cormorants, goosanders, otters and especially seals have all been blamed for compromising fishing interests but should we take at least some of the responsibility ourselves?

The colourful array of fishing boats in Scrabster Harbour twitch gently, their reflections cast perfectly in the tranquil water of a glorious spring morning. The mirror-calm sea lies flat and undisturbed save for the occasional surfacing of a grey seal scavenging for fish scraps.

Although Scrabster on Scotland's north coast is one of the top four landing ports in Britain, the thousand or more photographs that adorn the walls of the nearby Fishermen's Mission tell a story of a port which is unrecognisable with that of the past. Fading black and white images show the harbour packed with fishing boats, trading vessels and people. One picture from June 1899 shows a haul of 104 whales on the quayside with hundreds of onlookers clamouring around the harvest.

Ramsay Mackay was born and bred in Keiss, a small Caithness fishing village and has been fishing these waters for most of his years. He has witnessed many of the changes in the industry and understands as well as anyone the pressures facing today's coastal communities. We ask him about the local fishermen's feelings towards seals. "Obviously we don't like them," he says, "but we just accept them. They're not so much of a problem here but down the road in John O'Groats they might tell you different – they've got thousands there." Ramsay offers to show us the big bull grey seal that normally hangs around the harbour for hand-outs but he's not around today. "I usually throw him a fish or two – funny really."

Ramsay Mackay.

Predation on an industrialised scale.

Thirty miles north of Aberdeen on Scotland's east coast, Peterhead is the UK's leading whitefish port, landing around 40,000 tonnes a year. Pelagic landings (herring and mackerel) account for a further 90,000 tonnes. Like Scrabster, Peterhead has undergone many changes in its 400-year history but for the time being at least, seems to have found calm waters in the tumultuous sea of politics that has enveloped the fishing industry in recent times.

A long row of refrigerated trucks lines up outside Peterhead's state-of-the-art fish market shortly after 7am. Inside, activity is frantic as the

auctioneers lead their attendant band of buyers from one row of iced fish boxes to the next. In a language far removed even from broad Aberdonian dialect, each lot is quickly sold and loaded on board the waiting trucks. The process is industrialised and the volumes being moved reflect our own efficiency as marine predators. It is hard to imagine any significant competition from other species.

Yet fishermen up and down the country – from hard-pushed trawlermen to the hobbyist river angler – are often quick to blame a wide range of aquatic predators for declining catches. Every species from dolphins to kingfishers has been the scapegoat at one time or another and the conflict with unwelcome competition continues to simmer.

In a swish Aberdeen hotel we meet with Mike Park, Executive Chairman of The Scottish Whitefish Producers Association. Mike has been a skipper of a whitefish trawler for 30 years, although most of his time is now spent representing the industry he loves in endless meetings between London and Brussels. Last year alone, he clocked up more than 120 business flights. "If you had asked me about seals five years ago, you'd have got a very different answer. Back then, this industry was on its knees, fishermen were facing real hardship and they felt that no-one cared. They were being continually asked to reduce their catch and all they could see around them was more and more seals. It costs around £3m to put a whitefish vessel to sea and when it seems that nobody is listening, frustration kicks in. It's very hard to be green when you're in the red."

Mike knows what this hardship feels like but is not a man for languishing in the past. At the turn of the millennium, there were around 400 whitefish vessels in Scotland, now there are 120 with each boat covering an area of around 2,500 square kilometres. There has also been a 60% reduction in time spent at sea.

"During my time in this industry, things have changed dramatically," Mike continues. "All we used to be interested in was more fish, always fighting for more fish. Now we recognise the need to conserve stocks and we just want stability. At the moment, prices are up and generally the industry is in profit."

Mike is also acutely aware of the negative publicity that has followed the fishing industry in its calls for a cull on seals.

"These days, the industry has to manage its reputation and I tell my members not to get drawn into discussions about seals. We have become much more professional both at work and politically. The industry has grown up and we're taken much more seriously for that."

"IT'S VERY HARD TO BE GREEN WHEN YOU'RE IN THE RED."

As the rain hammers down in the city of granite, Mike has another meeting to attend. "To be honest, politics is our biggest threat today – there's no future for us in pointing the finger at seals. Mind you, if you said that to some of my members over a pint, they might not necessarily agree!" He laughs and runs out into the rain.

Britain's coastline supports internationally important populations of both grey and common (harbour) seals. The global population of greys is estimated at 350,000 with around 40% breeding in Britain. Although the 1980s and early 90s saw a rapid increase in grey seal numbers, recent research by the Special Committee On Seals, part of the National Environment Research Council, reports that grey seal pup production is now showing signs of stabilising. In 2005, an estimated 44,000 grey seal pups were born in Britain.

Estimates for common seals found in British waters number around 50,000–60,000. This represents approximately 40% of the European sub-species. It is believed however, that the population is in gradual decline but reasons are yet unclear.

Both species are protected by The Conservation of Seals Act 1970(COSA). The EU Habitats Directive (92/43/EEC) introduced in 1992, affords additional protection through designation of Special Areas of Conservation and more stringent restrictions on methods of taking or killing seals. The COSA presently allows for the shooting of any seal found in the 'vicinity' of fishing gear, although the Act does not define 'vicinity'. A wide range of marine conservation groups argue that in practice the law is unenforceable and that any seal, regardless of sex or age, can be killed with impunity. It is claimed that thousands are shot each year by fishing interests and that this is done indiscriminately, often resulting in wounding.

John Robins of Animal Concern: "The Conservation of Seals Act should be written on toilet paper as it offers seals no protection and gives those intent on killing seals almost total immunity. In 36 years, there has only been one successful prosecution under the Act."

Calls are increasingly being heard for a review of the legislation to bring it in line with laws relating to the conservation of other UK mammals. Libby Anderson of Advocates for Animals has been at the forefront of a campaign for a new Protection of Seals Act. "The present legislation is a relic of an era when attitudes to the killing of wild mammals were different and much less was known about the global importance of seals in UK waters," she says. Recent declines in the population of common seals in the Moray Firth, Shetland, Orkney and the Tay Estuary, support evidence that illegal killing of seals can impact on their conservation status.

"THE CONSERVATION OF SEALS ACT SHOULD BE WRITTEN ON TOILET PAPER AS IT OFFERS SEALS NO PROTECTION."

Marine mammals face a wide range of man-made hazards.

Between them, Britain's seals consume 220,000–395,000 tonnes of fish each year. A report by the Sea Mammals Research Unit (SMRU) at St Andrews University indicates that grey seals eat more than 8,000 tonnes of cod (4% of total stock) each year in the North Sea. This is four times the amount consumed 40 years ago.

Bertie Armstrong of the Scottish Fishermen's Federation said that an informed debate over reviving a cull of seals was needed. Ross Flett, Director of Orkney Seal Rescue countered: "We are the ones who should be adjusting our behaviour, rather than blaming seals."

The report exposed the raw nerve that is our inherent reluctance to share our natural resources. Whether seals seriously impact on industrial fishing or whether a greater threat is posed by our own over-

TOOTH & CLAW

exploitation, rests with individual perspectives but the debate over seal predation is not confined to the open sea.

Murray Stark is a lecturer at Inverness College but spends much of his time at a remote study centre on Loch Kishorn on Scotland's west coast. Murray has been involved in the salmon farming industry for 25 years and now teaches the practical side of aquaculture. "Seals have always killed salmon in cages," he says. "I've seen common seals kill 500 fish in one night." Although he no longer has a vested interest in commercial salmon farming, Murray is aware of the difficulties the industry has had to confront during its development. "As a fish farm manager in the past, you couldn't ignore predation of your stock. Whether you could do much that was effective is debatable. Seals are efficient hunters but not efficient feeders. They kill lots of fish but then leave them. From a fisherman's point of view, this is very wasteful."

As time has gone on, the salmon farming industry has developed various anti-predator mechanisms and become much more efficient in protecting its stocks. "Shooting seals was always ineffective," says Murray, "and it's not in the industry's interest to be looked upon as wholesale seal killers."

Murray's colleague is Bob Kindness who is in charge of fisheries research for the college. Following a sustained decline in both wild salmon and sea trout numbers, Bob captive-rears young fish to return to Scotland's river systems both for biodiversity and to improve rod-and-line catches. Both lecturers see the issue of predation as part of a much wider ecological picture.

"Nowadays we have the ability to catch an enormous amount of fish in the sea," says Bob. "In the last 40 years or so, fishing fleets have discovered the salmon's feeding grounds in the North Atlantic Ocean and although commercial fishing is now pretty insignificant, at its height, 3,000 tonnes were being caught each year. More recently, the massive take of mackerel in Norwegian waters is resulting in a high level of bycatch of young salmon, although again, solutions to this are presently being discussed."

With fewer salmon returning to their spawning rivers, the impact of predation is inevitably more pronounced. "Herons, cormorants and otters all take their toll and there are certainly 'rogue' seals who are venturing further up river systems," says Bob. "This sends out a warning about the state of the marine environment as a whole. If seals are exploring new areas, it suggests there are insufficient resources for them in the open sea."

Both men are pragmatic about controlling the impact of predation on wild fish stocks. Murray Stark: "Environmental groups remind us constantly of the power of nature to arrive at a balance. Given a healthy ecosystem, that's fine but that's not what we've got. Marine predators feed on different species so their adaptability allows them to prosper but prey species that are already threatened, remain under pressure by a disproportionate level of predation."

Bob thinks that having divorced ourselves from the rest of the animal kingdom, we're more sensitive to any intervention in the predation process. "The general public don't like the idea of animals being killed but it wasn't long ago that seals were seen as a resource, just like deer. Increasingly, people are uncomfortable with predator-prey processes, they can't relate to hunting – their hunting ground is the supermarket."

Murray intervenes. "We forget that Man is a top predator. We have played a crucial role in managing predator populations, we can't then suddenly decide that the best way to manage ecosystems is to walk away. If emotion is going to dictate the control of predators, I'm not sure this is necessarily in the best interests of all species."

The Wester Ross Fisheries Trust radio tagged 25 adult salmon to provide information on their movements. Eight (28%) were predated by otters. If this is representative, otter predation could be more significant even than sea lice in limiting salmon numbers.

"INCREASINGLY, PEOPLE CAN'T RELATE TO HUNTING – THEIR HUNTING GROUND IS THE SUPERMARKET."

Eider ducks have become unpopular with mussel farmers. In autumn, flocks of up to 500 can gather in sheltered coastal lochs. Each bird can eat 2kg of mussels in a day and is claimed to dislodge another 2kg. Some farmers claim they are literally being eaten out of business.

Although it's midsummer and the rest of Scotland is basking in warm sunshine, the wind is typically active in Kyle of Lochalsh, the last mainland town before you cross the bridge to the Isle of Skye. At the end of the jetty, *Seaprobe Atlantis*, one of the town's premier tourist attractions, bobs in the swell and even on a dreich west coast day, is an impressive, spotlessly clean and well-equipped vessel. Nigel Smith is the skipper and the local seals are one of his trump cards. "We carry around 10,000 visitors a year," he tells us, "and people love seeing the seals hauled out on the rocks."

Nigel Smith's business relies on the diverse wildlife to be found on Scotland's west coast and common seals are one of the main attractions for tourists. The sight of a seal wounded by gunshot reflects badly on the whole area and does nothing to enhance the public image of fish farming.

About a year ago, Nigel started noticing seal carcasses – not just one but several. He discovered that workers at the local salmon farm were shooting the seals. "I have no axe to grind with salmon farming," says Nigel, "but I do have a problem with indiscriminate shooting of seals by untrained marksmen. We saw one seal that hadn't been cleanly shot and was wounded."

It transpired that a local salmon farm had lost 3,000 fish from a hole in the cage. "Nobody could prove how the hole had appeared but on the basis that there was a hole, they started shooting seals. There was nothing scientific about it, it was more like revenge."

The company responsible decided that the negative publicity was costing them more than the fish so they replaced their anti-predator nets.

"I'm a pragmatist," says Nigel. "When I farmed, there was always the odd lamb or goose that got taken by a fox. If you live in the country, you have to accept that this happens. If a particular problem developed, I dealt with it. It didn't mean I went and shot anything that moved. People get so wrapped up in their own personal affairs, they lose perspective. If you don't look after your stock and it gets nicked, it's your own fault, yet we always blame the fox or the seal."

Some conservationists believe that seal shooting is widespread and that declines in common seal numbers reflect inadequate legislation to protect them.

"THERE WAS NOTHING SCIENTIFIC ABOUT IT, IT WAS MORE LIKE REVENGE."

During the summer, Peter Cunningham is a hard man to track down. Twenty years ago, rivers throughout Wester Ross were bulging with migratory salmon and sea trout, but not any more. The Wester Ross Fisheries Trust was established to monitor, conserve and enhance fish stocks in the region's rivers and Peter is the biologist employed to do just that. Today he is surveying the Glenmore River on the spectacular road to Glenelg using an innovative method to count the young fish in the river. By passing an electric current through the water using purpose-designed electro-fishing equipment, he can attract and catch juvenile fish, allowing them to be measured and to evaluate local populations in relation to previous years. Unlike some from the industry he represents, Peter feels that the impact of predators is only an issue because of low fish stocks.

A scientific approach to population dynamics provides answers to questions that were previously fed by anecdote alone.

Back in his office in the quiet coastal town of Gairloch, Peter makes a cup of tea and drops a huge pile of scientific reports on the table – clearly this is a well-researched subject. "The basic problem is that our ecosystems are all broken," he says. "There are bits that work but nothing is joined up. In the past, huge numbers of salmon would have meant that predators like bears, otters and foxes could all take their share. Half-eaten carcasses left on the bank would have returned nutrients to the soil – this would feed fresh vegetation growth which would improve riparian habitat for salmon and so it goes on. In this part of Scotland, the soils are deprived of phosphorus and this limits the fertility of bankside vegetation and subsequently food for fish."

Peter calls us over to the window and points to the distant hills. "Look, some tourists think this open landscape looks great but it really ought to be carpeted in vegetation supporting much more wildlife. It won't grow because the nutrients have all been washed away or removed faster than they have been replaced." Such views reflect an increasing appetite for a wider, longer-term, ecosystem approach to improving not only fish populations but a more robust habitat-based wildlife management regime, which will withstand natural predation. But this won't happen overnight and has yet to gain approval in the minds of a rural population understandably resistant to change.

"If fish stocks are high, predators are fine," Peter continues. "When stocks are low, some predators can contribute to the demise of local populations – it's simply a numbers thing."

A biological perspective is one thing but what about those at the sharp end? Ray Dingwall is River Manager for Poolewe Estates on the River Ewe. "I'm what they used to call a ghillie," he laughs. Ray's picturesque cottage sits on the banks of the Ewe and he's clearly still smitten by the lure of the river. "I've been fishing since I was five," he tells us. "We never used to give any thought to taking fish from the river." We ask him whether seals, otters and other predators make his job more difficult. "Everyone involved with salmon fishing has an opinion relating to fish stocks and fish health. I'm not one of these people who points the finger at this animal or that person. Every living thing has a place on this planet – the state of Scotland's fish stocks is a combination of many things."

Attitudes towards sport fishing have changed Ray explains, and whereas in years gone by anglers would take as much as they could, they're now much more conservation minded. "Education has played a big part in this change. Mind you, while we're putting our fish back, seals are wreaking havoc and being allowed to proliferate!"

"THE PROBLEM IS THAT OUR ECOSYSTEMS ARE ALL BROKEN."

The predation of wild salmon by seals has historically led to tensions between conservation interests and the rod-and-line fishery in Scotland. In 2005, widespread killing of seals prompted the funding of the Moray Firth Seal Management Plan (MFSMP). Professor Ian Boyd is Director of the Sea Mammals Research Unit (SMRU), the body responsible for the research. "Both salmon and seals are protected species and one eats the other so this requires some difficult value-judgements to be made," he says. Ian knows only too well how easily people make assumptions, and the belief that all seals eat salmon has undoubtedly resulted in seals being shot unnecessarily. "Data collected recently suggests that most seals feed well out to sea and that there may be relatively few individuals that feed on salmon."

The MFSMP research aims to establish the number of seals using certain river systems, identify those that are predating salmon to a significant degree and develop humane ways of mitigating their impact on fish returning to their spawning areas. Rob Harris is SMRU's man on the ground. "The plan has already been instrumental in reducing salmon and sea trout predation while also reducing the effects of management on the seal population. This

So-called 'problem' seals are identified over a period of time using photographic records although it is hoped that individual seals can be fitted with radio tags to learn more about their movements.

has been achieved by removing 'problem' seals through licensed shooting."

The Plan represents a landmark in co-operation between groups who were once in disagreement. Ian Boyd: "Seal predation is as much of a perceived problem as it is real. It is important to distinguish between the objective of maintaining a viable fishery, which is the focus of most salmon fisheries' managers, and the objectives of conserving salmon. For example, the presence of a seal in a river is enough to reduce the value of the fishing but only in certain circumstances will it have an impact on the salmon population. It is important to establish the scientific basis for managing seals in rivers so that we can achieve maximum effectiveness without compromising conservation objectives."

Whilst media attention has focused on the conflict between fishing interests and seals, populations of other aquatic predators have been recovering in recent decades and, with public sentiment and legislation stacked in their favour, disgruntled anglers find their hands are tied.

The artificial stocking of ponds and lakes is an open invitation to an opportunistic otter.

The recovery of the British otter population has been one of the most celebrated conservation success stories of recent times. Now firmly re-established across much of its natural range, the otter has become a totemic ambassador for mammals in the same vein as the osprey and red kite are for birds. *Tarka* is now held in great affection by the British public – a true paradox when one considers that only 50 years ago, otter hunts were still killing upwards of 1,000 animals each year. But their decline in the latter half of the 20th century – believed to be largely attributable to toxic insecticides entering our wetland systems – brought about a change in public attitude. Our tolerance, even affection, for predators is fickle and seemingly correlates strongly with their conservation status at any given time. 'Rare' and 'vulnerable' brings with it sympathy and protection whereas 'successful' and 'abundant' breeds contempt. The otter, like other recovering species, finds itself at a crossroads: its return being widely welcomed by the majority of observers but its increasing spread, edging it uncomfortably close to the 'too many' line for others.

A garden pond or stocked fishery is no different to an otter than peanuts are to a blue tit and they will happily accept the invitation to an easy meal. The Specialist Anglers Alliance (SAA) has claimed that stocks of prize fish are being devastated. A spokesman for the SAA said, "It can get very emotional seeing a specimen fish being taken by an otter."

For freshwater anglers, otters are not the only competition. Herons, goosanders and divers all eat fish and there is anecdotal evidence suggesting that even dippers are still persecuted for their impact on fisheries. But none of these species generates as much resentment from the angling community as the cormorant.

How long before questions are asked about the need to 'control' the growing osprey population? Our newly-found tolerance for wild nature is not universal nor is it unconditional.

Numbers of cormorants have increased substantially in recent decades, especially at inland water bodies. It is estimated that around 30,000 birds winter in Britain, 10,000 of these inland. Research suggests that in most areas, this is likely to increase further. Aggregate extraction and agri-environment schemes have created many new wetland systems and the artificial stocking of fish in these waters continues to fuel the cormorant's expansion.

There is no doubt that cormorants do predate fish that would otherwise be available to anglers but as with most facets of predator conflict, it is inappropriate to apply generalisations. Cormorant predation has been found to impact on fish stocks and, in some cases, biodiversity targets on a localised level but this varies over a period of time and is influenced by a myriad of other factors.

Like all wild birds, cormorants are protected by the Wildlife & Countryside Act 1981. Where 'serious damage' to fisheries can be proven, licences can then be granted for control. In 2003–4, 828 birds were licensed to be shot in England. In 2004, the Government revised the licensing requirements to shoot cormorants and removed the need to prove serious damage. The following season, almost 2,000 birds were licensed to be shot.

The value-judgements that determine the rights and wrongs of killing cormorants or seals are the same as those that influence perspectives on peregrine falcons or pine martens for their respective predation on racing pigeons and gamebirds. Is the apparent relaxation on licensing requirements for cormorants a precedent that represents the thin end of a wedge? Might this be used to legitimise calls for managing other 'problem' species? 'Management' is the contemporary euphemism for culling or control and the fundamental question remains: to manage or not to manage? And, if so, by what criteria and to whose benefit?

Three-quarters of Britain's households regularly put out food for garden birds. We would be disappointed if this investment failed to attract any visitors yet ironically, we are intolerant of the seal, otter or cormorant that is understandably attracted to a similar artificial food supply.

LIVING ON AN ISLAND

DOES CHARITY TOWARDS EUROPE'S LARGE CARNIVORES EXTEND TO HAVING THEM IN OUR OWN BACKYARD?

Throughout Europe, wolves, lynx and bears are ignoring political boundaries and are finding their way back to places where they have not been seen for decades. Our island status means that if we want these animals back, we have to physically bring them here. After centuries of living without them, is this a psychological barrier too far?

Although the rain is hammering on the overhead tarpaulin, spirits are high as another tray of German beer and wild boar hot-dogs is handed around. We're called over to an old leaking caravan in the corner of the field. Inside, it's dark and stuffy with everyone crammed in staring at a blank TV in the corner. Suddenly the screen bursts into life with some grainy pictures of three sand-coloured wolves padding along a forest track with a huge power station in the background. "You see, wolves don't need wilderness!" exclaims Gesa Kluth, a biologist working near Rietschen in eastern Germany, a small Saxony town just west of the Polish border.

Rietschen's landscape is unremarkable and not dissimilar to parts of rural England. Intensively managed forests give way to agricultural plains edged by grassy meadows, almost all of which accommodate a hunter's high seat. Cattle, horses and sheep graze in open pasture but the land lacks any defining features apart from the power station breaking the skyline. This is a functional landscape in which Rietschen's 3,000 residents work in farming, forestry, energy and tourism. Despite the uninspiring views, this is home for two resident wolf packs – the first to establish themselves in Germany since 1904.

The first wolves wandered across the border in 1998 and may have gone unnoticed had it not been for a killing spree one night when local shepherd Frank Neumann lost 33 sheep. Rumours abounded that the wolves had been planted – dropped at night from a helicopter – and in the face of a flurry of negative media, the government called on two young biologists, Gesa Kluth and Ilka Reinhardt, to investigate the wolf killings and liaise with the shepherd involved. Protective fencing was improved, compensation paid and the furore subsided. "It was important to protect the sheep but not to involve the shepherd with too much extra work," recalls Gesa. "This has been our policy ever since." The fact that Gesa and Ilka worked hard to help Frank Neumann has paid dividends and they've become good friends. "Shepherds are OK," says Gesa. "They don't love wolves but you can at least talk with them."

Frank is the host for tonight's impromptu barbeque and the two biologists, along with other local wildlife researchers, are part of the guest list. The video we are watching was filmed in a military area not far from Frank's farm. "I've never been completely opposed to wolves," he says, "but I cannot ever be their friend either. I haven't had a problem now for four years so I'm more relaxed and I have to say, wolves do fascinate me."

Gesa and Ilka now work full-time monitoring the two packs, collecting scats to analyse prey (Saxony's wolves eat mainly roe deer and wild boar), recording movements and investigating possible sightings. Although much of their work was initially focused on minimising livestock predation, this has become less of an issue recently.

"After eight years of wolves being back in Germany, hunters are the only problem," Ilka chimes in. "They want to control everything and see the wolves as competition for game. They won't listen, they won't talk and they don't want to know the facts. We have used their own statistics to illustrate that wolves are having no impact on game numbers but still they won't listen and several openly admit that if they see a wolf they will shoot it – in spite of a potential five year prison sentence." Ilka is visibly exasperated by the situation and concedes they have no idea how to proceed with hunters.

In Saxony, wildlife researchers and shepherds share an interest in their local wolves. It means they can work together to ensure that livestock casualties are kept to an absolute minimum.

Jana Schellenberg is the sole employee at the local *kontaktburo*, an information centre set up to provide up-to-date information about Saxony's wolves. Jana fields constant calls from the press, local residents and tourists wondering if they might catch a glimpse of a wolf. "Attitudes have changed enormously in the last two years," says Jana. "People are no longer afraid and they realise it's no big deal having the wolves around." There is a knock on the office door and an elderly gentleman bursts in gesturing excitedly. Our lack of German precludes us from the finer details but it seems obvious that the man has seen a wolf. Jana's diplomacy is impressive as she makes him a cup of tea. Given the circumstances, she politely suggests that the sighting was probably a large dog. The man is unconvinced and leaves still holding out his hands to show how big the wolf was. We're sure it's grown in size since he arrived.

"It is important that people learn about wolves and are kept informed of what they are doing locally," says Jana. "They will then form their own opinions but at least they have the facts." The *kontaktburo* delivers around 250 lectures each year to schools, business associations, hunting groups and tourism officials. It would seem that their efforts are paying off with around 50% of local residents feeling positively about the wolves and only 18% opposed to their presence. "The remainder don't care either way," laughs Jana.

A makeshift wolf information centre is soon to be replaced by a state-of-the-art exhibition. It would seem that most of Saxony's residents think that wolves are here to stay.

"The future of Saxony's wolves is in the balance," Ilka Reinhardt concludes. "They have produced healthy pups every year but those who leave the packs and stray outside the military area are not being seen again – I am sure they are being poached. If we are serious about having large carnivores in Germany, there needs to be the

Saxony's landscape is unremarkable. Germany's wolves don't need wilderness, they just need to be left alone.

political will to clamp down on this. At the moment, the hunters shout louder than wolf supporters and even though they are very much a minority in Germany, their voices are heard at a political level. Wolves can prosper here if we give them the chance."

Perhaps that chance will become more realistic through tourism revenue. At *Forsthaus Gasthof*, a quaint traditional guest house, owner Anita Szon is delighted with the wolves. "As the wolves come here from the East, the tourists come from the West!" she laughs.

The forest is silent save for the incessant buzzing of mosquitoes. Our small wooden hide, which has already been our home for six hours today, is dark and offers only a limited view of the pine forest outside. Suddenly, just before midnight, a huge male bear ghosts into the forest clearing – silently, without warning. He sniffs the air and eyes the hide suspiciously. Our scent will surely be masked by the stench of rotting pork from the pig carcass left out as bait. The bear starts to feed, cautiously at first then with one paw, he effortlessly rolls the carcass, which took three of us to drag into position. For a spine-tingling hour, the bear feeds just 20 metres from the hide. Finally sated with his bulging belly almost dragging on the floor, he fades away into the forest as silently as he arrived.

Lassi Rautiainen is passionate about two things: bears and saunas.

The following morning at breakfast, we meet up with Lassi Rautiainen, as close a resemblance to a northern Crocodile Dundee as you could imagine. Lassi is a celebrated wildlife photographer and one of several 'bear safari operators' in Eastern Finland taking advantage of the proximity of the Russian border and the bears who routinely cross from one side to the other. Lassi has eight hides positioned in the forest and accommodates around 200 guests each year. Every week throughout the summer he transports around 500kg of pig carcasses to his bait sites. They are unfit for human consumption and after several days of lying in the sun, it is surprising that the bears still find them appetising!

"Twenty years ago, people thought I was mad," says Lassi, "but now they can see money in bear tourism and everyone wants a slice." Lassi's guests include photographers, hunters, researchers, politicians and celebrities. To date, he has shown bears to people from 12 different countries. "It's just as much about education as entertainment," he says. "People who understand that bears will do them no harm have greater respect for them."

Not everyone is happy about Finland's bears being a tourist attraction. "Bear hunting is big in Finland – it's a status thing," Lassi tells us. "Sixteen bears have been illegally shot in this area in the last year. Hunters don't like me because my research on bear behaviour conflicts with the message they like to put out, which is that bears are dangerous and take livestock. They resent me challenging their views."

Lassi has never carried a gun with him in the forest. "Bears are very wary of people and this is healthy, both for us and the bears. I've no problem with carcasses being put out – it just supplements their natural food but we should never try to habituate them – this is when problems occur." For this reason, Lassi supports legal, regulated hunting. "It preserves the bear's fear of humans and apart from that, hunting is an exciting wild forest experience!"

"HUNTERS DON'T LIKE ME BECAUSE MY RESEARCH ON BEAR BEHAVIOUR CONFLICTS WITH THE MESSAGE THEY LIKE TO PUT OUT."

"PEOPLE WHO UNDERSTAND THAT BEARS
WILL DO THEM NO HARM HAVE
GREATER RESPECT FOR THEM."

Europe's three apex predators – bear, wolf and lynx – are all on the increase and are finding their way into places where they have not been seen for tens, even hundreds of years. Their absence has meant that local people have had ample opportunity to get used to life without them.

The spread of large carnivores in Europe has resulted from a combination of natural dispersal and deliberate reintroductions but their reappearance is not always welcome. According to John Linnell of the Large Carnivore Initiative for Europe (LCIE), depredation on livestock is the most widespread conflict and problems are most severe when predators return to an area after a long absence. "People who are used to their presence generally get along with them, but those that are not, have forgotten how to share their living space with these predators."

Europe has collectively committed to protect and conserve its large carnivores which include wolf, bear, wolverine and both Eurasian and Iberian lynx. The EU Habitats Directive provides the legal framework for their management and Article 22 of the Directive 92/43, requires that all member states examine the desirability of reintroducing formerly native species where their demise resulted from the actions of people. Britain is party to this legislation. Our legal obligation aside, many contest that we have a moral responsibility to play our part in re-accommodating those species that in less enlightened times we persecuted to extinction.

Back in Germany, Gesa Kluth is pragmatic about the possible return of wolves to Britain. "If you have wolves you will always have problems – it is intrinsic in the relationship between people and wolves today. But they are also fascinating animals and can bring huge benefits. The challenge is to balance that out and that is much easier when the wolves move in on their own four feet." None of the species that fall within the scope of the legislation can ever do this in Britain and so, if we want them back, we have to pick them up and physically bring them here.

"IF SOCIETY WANTS WOLVES IN GERMANY, THEY MUST BE PREPARED TO PAY FOR ANY DAMAGE THEY CAUSE." GESA KLUTH

In recent years, Britain has pioneered species reintroductions with the successful return of the sea eagle, red kite and osprey (to England). The scientific and logistical knowledge required to effect this was hard-won but we now have the opportunity – and potentially the legislative obligation – to reintroduce other species that once lived here. But is it really feasible to restore large carnivores to an island with 60 million people and an eclectic mix of demands on a diminished countryside? Is there enough space? What will they eat? Who should make the decisions? Why bother?

Alan Watson Featherstone is Executive Director of Trees For Life (TFL), a Scottish charity dedicated to restoring the Caledonian Forest to large parts of the Highlands. "We need to adopt a different attitude towards the use of land," says Alan. "Ecologically, we are still mining it and there is a perceived need for all land to be productive. We need to understand that nature is not there simply for us to exploit." TFL have been planting and protecting native trees in Scotland for almost 20 years but Alan is quick to point out that their work is about more than just trees. "A forest is a jig-saw puzzle that must be complete, with all its constituent species, before it can function efficiently. We need to build an irrefutable case for ecological considerations to predominate over economics."

The proposed reintroduction of the European beaver to Scotland's wetlands has

Getting reacquainted with an unfamiliar neighbour that many perceive as a real threat to our own safety would involve a huge shift in cultural and political mindset. But will the price of an incomplete ecosystem be even higher for those who follow the present generation of decision makers?

TOOTH & CLAW

been a protracted and politically complex issue which remains unresolved. Britain is one of only three European countries that has not restored beavers. The political wranglings that have put a stranglehold on beaver reintroduction send out a clear signal about the difficulties in considering the return of large predators.

"The return of the beaver is critical," says Alan emphatically. "This would be the first terrestrial species that we've reintroduced in modern history and would act as a stepping stone for others. I would envisage lynx returning within 20 years – it could happen much sooner given a change in perspectives. This needs to be brought about by educating children, who will be the decision makers in 20 years. I'll be disappointed if there are no wild wolves in Scotland before I die."

Many Norwegian farmers are also passionate hunters and competition for game is largely unwelcome.

Zanete Andersone-Lilley has researched ecology and public perceptions of large carnivores for more than ten years in her native Latvia. Her childhood memories are of wandering in the forest with her tiny dog picking berries and mushrooms. She can recall at an early age seeing a sheep badly injured by wolves but this was a reality people lived with and Zanete can remember being far more afraid of sheep than of wolves! Having now lived in southern England for a couple of years, Zanete finds it hard to envisage how society here would adapt to large predators. "Britain is too over protective," she says. "People are alienated from nature, they don't see themselves as part of it anymore, hence it is regarded as dangerous, something to be controlled."

During her work in Latvia, a country where like many in Eastern Europe, hunting is an integral part of rural life, Zanete was often asked how many wolves should be allowed to live in the country. Realising that managing wolves was actually about managing people's attitudes, her standard response was: "As many as we can tolerate."

Zanete has recently moved to Norway where there are said to be more wolf researchers than there are wolves. This, in stark contrast to neighbouring Sweden where large carnivores are a conservation priority and are being encouraged to spread into areas beyond their heavily-forested strongholds.

"PEOPLE ARE ALIENATED FROM NATURE, THEY DON'T SEE THEMSELVES AS PART OF IT ANYMORE, HENCE IT IS REGARDED AS DANGEROUS, SOMETHING TO BE CONTROLLED."

We spoke to a Norwegian researcher familiar with human-predator issues. He asked not to be named because of the highly charged nature of the predator debate. "Farmers are the most single influential lobby group in Norwegian politics," he told us. "The result is that the government has set a ceiling of only three breeding wolf packs in the country. This is what they call a sustainable population."

We ask if it is possible for a single-interest group to gain so much sway that they dictate national policy. "Dictate might be a bit strong but a decisive preponderance of influence would be a fair summary," he tells us. "The kernel of this is not so much about wolves or lynx but about control of rural Norway. Farmers receive a basic subsidy here, equivalent to the salary of an average industrial worker and they are aware that politically this is a precarious position so they feel insecure, even paranoid. Predator politics gets dragged into their fight to retain both their income and status."

Some of our contact's research colleagues have been accused of conspiracy against Norwegian farmers by deliberately releasing wolves under the cover of darkness. The strength of feeling is so strong that some researchers have even received death threats.

In January 2006, the Norwegian government was asked to sanction the killing of one of Norway's two remaining wolf packs on the grounds that local people were afraid and their mental health was suffering. On this occasion, the request was denied when wolf supporters pointed out that by the same logic, anyone afraid of flying should be able to have the local airport closed down!

Each year, Norway sets a quota for lynx hunting. Such is the appetite to bag a prestigious trophy, the season is normally over within a couple of days.

"I'll be disappointed if there are no wild wolves in Scotland before I die."

Not the stuff of tea parties perhaps but Europe's brown bears generally regard us as the predator. As with any large animal, respect is a must but fear comes easily when you're not used to having them around.

There is no doubt that these charismatic creatures capture our imagination and release deep-seated emotions. The most famous predator of 2006 was undoubtedly Bruno the Bear who nonchalantly wandered across the Austrian border into Germany where he started to kill sheep and explore human settlements. He was the first wild bear in Germany since 1835 and the media prioritised his progress over the national football team's World Cup campaign.

Bruno was identified as 'JJ1', the offspring from two bears that were part of a reintroduction project in Italy. His mother had been known to be a bear accustomed to visiting villages and once he became independent, Bruno continued this behaviour. For over a month, Bruno evaded capture from some of the most experienced bear hunters in Europe but on 26th June 2006, he was shot near the town of Zell in southern Germany. Bruno's killing provoked intense reaction that saw members of the public filing legal complaints against the Bavarian Ministry, memorial websites being set up and Bruno becoming immortalised in a range of collectable teddy bears.

One newspaper reporter summed up the frustration of many people. "Our inability to co-exist with nature has yet again prompted us to reach for the trigger." Heike Finke, spokeswoman for Germany's Wildlife Alliance told newspapers, "I have to go and lecture developing world countries about how they should save their lions and tigers. I haven't got much credibility as a German when we kill our only bear."

Predators take us on an emotional roller coaster. Clearly, life alongside wolves, bears and lynx is not without its challenges, even in places where they have always existed. For countries like Britain, the difficulties – real and perceived – are even greater but we can at least observe the experiences of other countries and learn from their mistakes. It really comes down to the one question, the same question that is being asked of people all over the world: do we want to share our space with large carnivores and if so, under what conditions? The answer depends on personal priorities and the value that a society places on the natural world. Conserving predators is all about human psychology.

In recent years, improved understanding of the importance of ecosystem dynamics along with changing land-use priorities in rural areas, has fuelled calls for the return of wolves to Britain, or more specifically to the Scottish Highlands. For some time, there has been increasing concern over high densities of red deer in certain areas and their impact on already impoverished ground vegetation. In the absence of any natural predators – other than Man – deer have proliferated and wolves have been suggested as one way of restoring the population to a level more in keeping with the carrying capacity of their habitat.

Before any consideration can be given to restoring species such as the wolf, legislation requires a public consultation to determine how desirable such a move would be. Not surprisingly, several researchers have recently looked into public attitudes towards large predators.

A recent survey shows that generally speaking, the Scottish public are positive towards species reintroductions, including wolves. There is more support from those living in urban environments but even individual farmers working in areas where wolf reintroduction has been discussed, were only slightly less positive to the idea. The most vociferous opposition came from the organisation that represented those farmers.

In another survey, 66% of respondents were supportive of returning wolves to Scotland, a figure which is higher than in countries where reintroductions have already been carried out. This particular survey included interviews with tourists who displayed greater support than local residents, reinforcing the claim that it is much easier to conserve large predators from a distance.

Wolves and bears are headline grabbers and tend to hijack discussions over predator restoration in Britain. But what of the lesser-known lynx? Dr David Hetherington has researched the feasibility of reintroducing Eurasian lynx to Scotland and is anxious to distance himself from discussions over the two larger carnivores. "Lynx suffer in perception terms by being linked with wolves," says David, "when in fact they are very different animals. Probably the biggest obstacle to lynx reintroduction here is that people don't know much about them."

There have already been successful lynx reintroductions into France, Switzerland, Slovenia and the Czech Republic. Populations are also being reintroduced into parts of Germany and Poland. Lynx are solitary, ambush predators often occupying home ranges up to 1,000 square kilometres and preying predominantly on small and medium-sized woodland deer. David Hetherington's research suggests that there is sufficient habitat and prey to support around 400 lynx in the Scottish Highlands and a further 50 in the Southern Uplands.

So is this elusive feline a threat to livestock and are they dangerous to humans? David offers a considered response. "Comparing Scotland with similar models of livestock husbandry elsewhere, I would say that there will be some sheep predation but levels will be low and localised. It is also possible to mitigate those losses, as has been done in Switzerland where the total number of sheep lost to lynx in 2006 was just 15. People certainly shouldn't be afraid of lynx as they are extremely wary of humans and they don't go looking for trouble with dogs, unlike wolves. A mother lynx with young would not be aggressive to humans – she would back off."

Even where lynx have healthy populations, they are rarely seen.

David is clearly passionate about seeing this charismatic creature returned to his native land but his reasons are practical rather than romantic. "You could argue that we have a basic, ethical obligation to restore a species that we hunted to extinction but that aside, this country has no top predators, other than humans. There is nothing that routinely kills woodland deer and lynx do this all year round taking both males and females, young and old – this is much more natural than culling by humans. When lynx leave a carcass in the forest, an array of scavenging invertebrates benefit and nutrients are returned to the soil. Lynx also kill smaller predators, especially foxes. There is an economic side to this too – lynx not only help to control woodland deer numbers, they are a huge tourism draw. People associate an area that has lynx as wild and beautiful because lynx are wild and beautiful. They add a mystique to the forest."

Perfect lynx habitat.

Whilst the rest of Europe wrestles with the challenges of increasing predator populations, Britain can sit back safe in the knowledge that our countryside is free from such hazards. Or can it?

In a remote glen in north-west Scotland, the local red deer population has just been reduced by three. Innes MacNeill, head ranger on Alladale Wilderness Reserve, is strapping the lifeless bodies of three dead hinds to his ponies ready for the long trek down the hill. It's January and stalkers throughout Scotland will be out culling hinds but the motivation to reduce deer numbers at Alladale is slightly different.

In 2003, this 25,000 acre traditional sporting estate was bought by Paul Lister, a man with a vision. Drawing on inspiration from his visits to Yellowstone's self-regulated ecosystems and his trips to the up-market ecotourist lodges of South Africa, he conceived the idea of creating the northern hemisphere's first Africa-style game reserve, complete with formerly extirpated species such as bear, lynx and wolf. Reducing deer numbers to facilitate regeneration of the natural forest, is the first step in realising this vision.

Back at the recently refurbished lodge, now providing luxury accommodation for wilderness retreats, Paul passionately explains his mission. "Scotland's wildlife is pretty good but to be taken seriously as a major wildlife tourism destination, we need certain species. People go to Africa and yes, they want to see the birds and grazing animals but it's lions, leopards and cheetahs that really fires them up – people want to see carnivores. Yellowstone is a place where you can prove that people will travel miles to see large predators. The same thing can happen in Alladale."

Alladale Wilderness Reserve in Sutherland.

Paul's plan is to enclose a huge area of land with a sophisticated electric fence, creating a fully-functioning but controlled ecosystem. He is insistent that this is not an official predator reintroduction. "Alladale may well become a stepping-stone to the return of other species but

A packed Community Hall in Ardgay near Alladale eagerly listen to Paul Lister's plans.

this is not what we set out to achieve. As long as people keep livestock and pets, I don't see wolves and bears as an option in the wild and I want to do something that can actually happen."

Paul believes Alladale will become the leading wildlife attraction in the UK and sees this as a major opportunity to revitalise stagnant areas of the Scottish Highlands. "No amount of ecological evidence will persuade government to bring back troublesome species like large carnivores, it's down to job opportunities and financial sustainability."

A hundred miles east, Keith Marshall and Anke Fischer are enduring a summer heatwave in their Aberdeen office. Both are part of the Socio-Economic Research Programme (SERP) at the Macaulay Institute. Their work explores various aspects of our relationship with wildlife and landscapes. Both researchers feel that decisions about reintroducing large predators should be based on the same principles that inform other wildlife management. "Local stakeholder involvement is crucial," says Keith. "People do not respond well to being excluded from the decision-making process. They are more likely to adopt new ideas if they are listened to and their concerns addressed. It is a question of respect."

Anke adds, "I don't think the views and opinions of ecologists should be set apart from those of the general public. Their value-judgements may be based on different criteria but this doesn't make their views necessarily any more objective than those based on social, cultural or economic factors – ecologists are just people too, often with their own agendas."

Both Anke and Keith concede that the issues surrounding predator restoration are complex. "The process needs professional and independent mediation, which is a skill that is rarely included in wildlife policy discussions."

So in reality, what are the chances of wolves, lynx and bears once again stalking the forests and mountains of a country whose landscape is unrecognisable from a time when they were last here? Inverness is the capital of Highland Scotland and is the new headquarters for Scottish Natural Heritage (SNH), the government's advisory body who would be charged with investigating the implications of returning such species. Martin Gaywood is their Species Action Framework Manager. "We're not presently considering the reintroduction of large carnivores as, under IUCN guidelines, public support needs to be established and we remain unconvinced of any significant appetite to see these animals returned. We are also required to determine whether the original reason for the species' demise has been removed. In the case of large carnivores, this was human persecution and without public support, we consider that this threat could still be present."

It appears that although discussions over returning large carnivores to Britain are gathering momentum, the political will to move the process forward lacks any conviction. For the moment at least, it seems that we remain part of the Union in name only.

The final word should perhaps go to Doug Smith, Head of the Yellowstone Wolf Recovery Project in USA, who has spent 24 years dealing not only with wolves but with the people who both love and loathe them. "I think we need to quit talking about just wolves or bears and look at the bigger picture. With all the growing problems in the world, we need to start talking about nature as a whole, how valuable it is and yet, at times, how fragile it is."

"PEOPLE ARE MORE LIKELY TO ADOPT NEW IDEAS IF THEY ARE LISTENED TO AND THEIR CONCERNS ADDRESSED. IT IS A QUESTION OF RESPECT."

THE FEELGOOD FACTOR

PREDATORS – A REMEDY FOR NATURE DEFICIT DISORDER?

As we become further isolated from our roots, we seek solace in the material wealth by which our lives are now measured. Yet for an increasing number of people, this is not enough: they need contact with nature. A close encounter with a top-of-the-food-chain predator is something that stays with you forever. Do we see something of our wild past in these animals? Do we empathise with their struggle for survival? One thing is beyond question: they make us feel good!

There are no signs indicating that this is the place. No visitor centre, gift shop or toilets. Neither is it particularly scenic. But there is something that's brought the 50 or so onlookers to this shingle spit just outside Inverness. An unspoken understanding. A handful of people are stood right by the waterline as the tide pushes its way up the beach. The rest are sitting soaking up the afternoon sun. Many come here almost every day.

At first, a few dorsal fins break the smooth surface every minute or so. Occasionally, one of the dolphins tosses a salmon through the air and a rumbling of appreciation ripples through the gathering. Then without warning, two bottle-nosed dolphins – sleek and glistening in the sunshine – simultaneously leap clear of the water just 20 metres from a spellbound audience. Cries of excitement fill the air followed by a very British round of applause – the only way that we can thank the dolphins for their entertainment. For the next 20 minutes, a dozen or so dolphins exuberantly chase the migrating fish caught in the currents just offshore. Every now and then, one jumps clear of the sea, then another and another. There is a smile etched on the face of every person present. They have fallen under the spell of these most northerly of bottle-nosed dolphins and are experiencing *biophilia*.

Edward O. Wilson, a Harvard University entomologist, coined the term *biophilia* which refers to our innate love of life. Wilson proposed the possibility that the deep affiliations we humans have with nature are rooted in our biology. The *biophilia hypothesis* suggests that there is an instinctive bond between human beings and other living systems and that humans evolved as creatures inextricably linked to the intricacies of nature and that we still have this affinity ingrained in our genotype.

It makes sense. For 10,000 generations, we had to survive without all the trappings of modern-day life. No mobile phones, no cars, no computers, no retail parks. We evolved with the much more simple requirements of food, water, shelter and safety. In just a few short generations, we have turned our backs on nature and no longer need the life-supporting services it previously provided. Or so we think.

Wilson proposes that although our perceptions of our natural environment have been refined, we are still fundamentally attracted to all that is alive and vital, and subconsciously seek out connections with wild nature. Predators are a particularly spectacular facet of that nature and that's why they are such a draw.

Enveloped by the early morning mist we follow in the deliberate footsteps of Jani Maatta as he makes his way along the well-worn path to the hide, hidden deep in the forest. All is quiet as we arrive but that immediately changes as we open the large wooden door. After 12 hours sitting in one place, the 20 or so bear watchers inside are grateful to stretch their legs and get some fresh air but did they see any bears?

The smile on the face of James Silverthorne, a photographer from England, suggests that they have. "Bloody brilliant!" he says. "We had cubs climbing trees, males fighting. There seemed to be bears everywhere. It was just non-stop!" We're joined by several Brits who have travelled to the Martinselkonen Wilds Centre in eastern Finland as part of a group. "Nineteen different bears," says one lady emphatically. "I'm sure I counted 21," says another. Different accounts of how many bears were seen and what they all did, echo around the forest in several different languages as the eclectic group makes its way back to the lodge for breakfast.

Karhu is Finnish bear beer and is a well-known method of increasing the number of bear sightings!

It takes a bit of effort to see a brown bear in Europe but more and more people are making that effort. More and more people want to see predators in their natural environment – polar bears, killer whales, sea eagles. These are animals that make the blood course through our veins. We find these animals exciting, they make us feel alive. For most of us, even the briefest glimpse of a predator is uplifting. A fox crossing the road on our way to work; a sparrowhawk dashing past our window in a blur; a seal momentarily surfacing in a coastal harbour. These are things that brighten up our day. They make us feel good. Edward Wilson's *biophilia* is contagious.

As the pressures facing the natural world become daily more acute, so the political lobbying over the future of our countryside, and the management of the species which depend upon it, becomes more intense. Slick advertising campaigns using emotional imagery and selective statistics garner support for single-interest groups. Shrouded in contemporary euphemisms, the self-serving agendas which drive much of the predator debate give little credence to intangible concepts like *biophilia*. But scientific evidence is evolving to suggest that such notions – previously regarded as frivolous and woolly – may well underpin all that we deem to be important in our lives. For most of our history, we've shared the same struggles for survival as other species still do, but now at a time when on a material level most of us want for nothing, is there something missing in our lives? Without realising it, are we spiritually homesick for the wild environment: our natural home?

In a recent report which explored the link between wild nature and our own well-being – physical, spiritual and financial – the President of the European Commission, Jose Manuel Barroso, concluded: "Biodiversity is integral to sustainable development, it underpins competitiveness, growth and employment, and improves livelihoods. Biodiversity loss, and the consequent decline of ecosystem services, is a grave threat to our societies and economies." Through a series of case studies throughout Europe, the report highlighted the strong links between biodiversity protection, social cohesion, economic growth and human well-being.

For the third time, the young pine marten peers suspiciously over the wall at the end of the garden. She's been here several times already this week but always with her mother. This time, it appears she's alone. We sit on the grass hardly daring to move as bit by bit she ambles up the garden towards us. A distant dog bark causes her to stop and for a moment, it looks like she'll make off but she keeps coming. Now, only a matter of metres from our feet, our host Gordon Thomas bends forward and offers the young marten a raisin from his hand. Surely such a rare and elusive wild animal will decline the invitation? She is reluctant at first but sniffs at the food, then gently takes it from him. In a second she is gone and the show is over.

Gordon has been feeding *his* pine martens in his Argyll garden for several years and sits for hours watching them cavort on the lawn and in the trees. This year's offspring – or the one we saw at least – are bolder than any he's seen before. "There can't be many places in the world where you can hand-feed a wild pine marten like that," beams Gordon. "I never tire of seeing them." His voice betrays an obvious emotional attachment to these animals.

Although the evidence to support the link between our health and the natural environment is still evolving, another report commissioned by the RSPB suggests that nature does in fact have a quantifiable health value and that contact with wildlife-rich areas may be a significant component in addressing a wide range of mental and social health issues. The author of the report, Dr William Bird, points out that neither technology nor cities can replace our innate need for nature. In disconnecting ourselves from the natural environment we have become strangers to that world: the world from which we evolved.

The social fractures that accompany our modern lifestyles are apparent. More than 40,000 British children are now taking anti-depressants. In 2002, almost 45,000 young people under the age of 25 attempted suicide. A recent study placed Britain twenty-first out of 25 European states for the well-being of its children and a recent BBC survey showed that we were happier in the 1950s than we are today, despite a threefold increase in wealth. With governments struggling to find solutions to major problems like obesity, depression, stress and anti-social behaviour, can we really afford to ignore the possibilities offered by the very environment that shaped what we are?

It might not be cool to admit it but we all need nature.

TOOTH & CLAW

"THE ONE PROCESS NOW GOING ON THAT WILL TAKE MILLIONS OF YEARS TO CORRECT IS THE LOSS OF GENETIC AND SPECIES DIVERSITY BY THE DESTRUCTION OF NATURAL HABITATS. THIS IS THE FOLLY OUR DESCENDANTS ARE LEAST LIKELY TO FORGIVE US."

EDWARD O. WILSON

At the end of a leafy lane in Bedfordshire, a parking lot overlooks a small collection of enclosures fitted out with high-wire fences, powerful spotlights and an array of state-of-the-art security cameras. The scene can only be described as something reminiscent of a prison camp. Phil Watson is chairman and founder of the Anglian Wolf Society and the prison-style enclosures are, in fact, home for six socialised wolves. One of the society's objectives is to give people the chance to be close to wolves in a controlled environment and to learn about them and from them. Phil recounts a particularly moving tale.

"One child came here with his school and had a real problem with wolves – he'd had really vivid nightmares about them from an early age. His parents were keen for him to confront his fear. At first, he wouldn't come anywhere near the wolves but as I started to talk to the group, he began to relax. We then took the wolves out for a walk and finally, the little boy slowly reached out a hand and let a fully-grown adult wolf walk past him, its fur brushing through his fingers. There was some sort of emotional spark from within and the child just came to life. He ended up with his arms around the wolf's neck sobbing his heart out. Now his bedroom is plastered with wolf posters!"

A supervised visit to a zoo might tick the relevant box on the school curriculum but many of these inner-city children would likely swap this for an hour running free in the countryside.

The emotional spark to which Phil refers has been lit elsewhere but in altogether more grave circumstances. In 1998, Troy Bennett was working as a shepherd in a livestock cooperative in the high Alps between Italy and France. One night in summer, 280 sheep were herded over a cliff. Troy describes the scene: "Some of the sheep were still alive, wounded and bleeding. Some were hanging onto the cliff edge, some had got caught on trees whilst falling. It was carnage."

During the following week, Troy was asked to gather the remaining sheep from the mountains. As he wandered the ridges with his young son, he discovered more dead sheep, some partially eaten. He carried one wounded animal back down the mountainside and as darkness descended, there in the trees only five metres ahead, a wolf stood staring back at him.

"Our eyes met and were locked," he recalls. "When a wolf looks into your eyes, you cannot look away. And in that look, I felt something change; I felt an exchange of information. I don't know what the wolf took from it but I was left with something – a gift that has stayed with me."

It is difficult to pinpoint exactly what it is about predators that draws us in. Somewhere deep inside us we are instinctively excited by their presence. Science cannot measure it and political policy is reluctant to acknowledge it, but it is undoubtedly real. If we are prepared to accept that nature is not only good for us but is an essential component of our future lives, then we must surely accept nature as a complete ecological package – we cannot pick and choose those bits that suit us and discard the rest. In Aldo Leopold's words. 'If the land mechanism as a whole is good, then every part is good'.

Predators are not always welcome as part of that package. The concerns of those affected by expanding predator populations are both real and legitimate. Living alongside growing numbers of wild animals that influence our lives on many different levels is a new thing for us, something we're not used to. It is unreasonable and naive to expect a universal welcome for species that are changing the landscape and, perhaps more significantly, our attitudes and policies towards that landscape. It may be the change itself that is most alien but there is surely no future in dismissing understandable opposition to this change.

Twenty-first century Britain offers the opportunity to experience exciting predators at close range for the first time in modern history. Red kites once again quarter the skies over both town and country. Ospreys no longer bypass England on their way to their Scottish strongholds – they are stopping and establishing territories, every year in new areas. Sea

eagles, one of the largest raptors in the world, are spreading from Scotland's remote west coast and being returned to other favourable habitats. Expanding grey seal colonies in eastern England are becoming major tourist attractions and peregrine falcons, the fastest creatures on earth, are nesting in the heart of our busy cities.

Shifting motivations and priorities within society have brought about this change in predator fortunes. Recent years have seen a transformation in what predators mean to people and that process continues, bringing with it conflicting viewpoints on how or whether predator populations should be managed in the future. There are many entrenched positions – all hiding behind their respective fences. The mud-slinging that then characterises the stereotyping of different

interest groups – bobble hats, bunny-huggers, gamies, toffs and worse
– does nothing to further constructive dialogue. The secret surely lies in
taking the fences away.

How easily this can be achieved will ultimately depend on the value
society places on the role of predators in our lives. This is different for
everyone and depends on the criteria used, but in considering the
wider, longer-term outlook for future generations, should we not avoid
the temptation to always measure the worth of other species in terms
of what they can produce for our balance sheets? Can we afford to
miss the opportunities offered in accommodating the 'nature package'
not only within our physical space but within our hearts and minds?

There are many challenges facing the human species, some of which
we show a worrying reluctance to address seriously. There is presently
a generation moving through our education system, which will in
many areas be deprived of the simple, wondrous prompts of nature
that children of the past could take for granted. True, they have access
to more theoretical learning than ever before but many will reach
adulthood without ever having had soil under their finger nails and
with little or no contact with wildlife. If we cannot engage and excite
this generation about their natural environment, we cannot reasonably
expect these adults of tomorrow to find relevance and value in it.

In this context, the political, social, cultural and economic issues that
today hang like a cloud over discussions on predator management are
insignificant. Unless our young people are allowed to reconnect with
nature and intuitively understand the natural processes that link all life
together, future perceptions of predators are likely to continue to be
dogged by socio-politics rather than by ecology and our own well-
being.

Human tolerance, or the lack of it, has always been the dominant fact
of life for Britain's predators. But whilst we continue to determine
which species are allowed to prosper and those that are not, humans
also have much at stake. We hope that this book will encourage
everyone affected by predators to remember this. If we all take the time

TOOTH & CLAW

to re-examine our perspectives; to question our fears, prejudices and inconsistencies, it is apparent that in nature's plan there is no such thing as a good or bad animal. There are only those animals that kill to eat – predators, and those that are killed and eaten – prey.

The kitchen door bursts open and my young son stands there breathless. "There's a red kite over the house," he gasps. Having never seen a red kite in our area, I'm confident that Sam has misidentified a buzzard but my wife and I go out to take a look. There, soaring against a vivid blue sky, is the unmistakable silhouette of a kite. "Told you," says Sam, smiling.

T&C SELECTED OPINIONS

To gain an insight into how the British public feel about different facets of human-predator conflict, we set a number of questions which require value-judgements to be made. The *Tooth & Claw* website has received thousands of responses to these questions – the following pages reveal some of them.

Sparrowhawks are medium-sized birds of prey. They have increased in numbers over recent decades following an extensive decline. They kill and eat garden birds such as blue tits and robins. Do you think their numbers should be controlled to protect garden birds?

Yes 19%   No 70%   Don't know 11%

- Predation is a fact of life. Many garden birds are predators in their own right but their prey e.g. insects are not thought of as cute, whereas the sparrowhawk is preying on animals which are familiar and emotive.

- The presence of sparrowhawks is indicative of a healthy ecosystem, and I am thrilled to see sparrowhawks in and around my garden.

- I am someone who keeps racing pigeons, but would not like to see predators unnaturally controlled. The prey will always outnumber the predator.

- If you increase the number of garden birds by feeding as I do then we must expect small bird predators to exploit this.

- Raptors are relatively small in numbers but can have a devastating effect if their numbers are not controlled.

- Yes it definitely needs something done. It is not unusual to see a sparrowhawk pluck while still alive – collared doves, a woodpecker (once), starlings and sparrows (I don't mind) and the odd partridge.

- In the 60s the predator-prey balance was upset by pesticides. It has taken many years for them to recover, so the base line for population dynamics should be not be based purely on population increases in recent years.

- Sparrowhawks have destroyed some song bird populations and have overbred out of proportion.

- Scientific research suggests that declining small bird species is due to the loss of habitat and food. Removing sparrowhawks will do nothing but appease those misguided enough to blame them for the problem.

- We should not keep interfering with the food chain for sentimental reasons and our greed.

- Predation should help to improve the overall fitness of garden bird populations.

- They are exterminating our garden birds which we feed and look after.

- I enjoy birdwatching very much. A sparrowhawk visits our garden and it is a nuisance. I have seen it catch our garden birds and it is very upsetting.

- This is part of the natural ebb and flow of nature: they were previously common and have made a comeback, we should celebrate this.

Red grouse inhabit the upland moors of northern England and large parts of Scotland. They support significant rural employment through landowners selling grouse shooting rights. Hen harriers are a bird of prey that feed on red grouse as well as other upland birds. They are protected by law but some grouse moor owners would like their numbers controlled to protect their shooting interests. Do you agree with them?

Yes 21%   No 69%   Don't know 10%

- Killing magnificent birds because they eat other birds that humans want to momentarily keep alive so they can shoot them instead is the most absurd thing I've ever heard!

- Rural livelihoods are important and shooting generates more income for the economy than birdwatching ever will.

- Grouse moors are highly beneficial to other species and who will pay for their upkeep if the grouse shooting declines?

- We need to protect the wealth of upland waders and other birds that inhabit grouse moors. Without the grouse the habitat management would not exist.

- Grouse numbers have declined hugely over the last 200 years, not as a result of predation, but of disease and mismanagement of the moors.

- Killing birds of prey is (yet more) very bad PR for rural areas which really need support and understanding from the taxpayer.

- No one wants to see hen harriers eliminated...just controlled.

- Hunting for sport or trophies is becoming less and less socially acceptable. As a society, we should look for alternative ways of providing rural employment.

- A quota system on hen harriers would allow conservationists and land managers to agree on policies to benefit ALL bird species.

- A healthy red grouse population should be able to withstand the predation of hen harriers.

- Harriers have far more right to be there than any human with a gun.

- Relocation, rather than control, is one possibility, as is a compensation payment to moors for each successful harrier nest.

- I have been an active part in grouse shoots before and it is a real pleasure to see a hen harrier or a short-eared owl on the shoot.

- There are probably more grouse left to die a cruel lingering death after being injured by a bad shot than those which are taken by hen harriers.

Capercaillie are our largest grouse, emblematic of the ancient pinewoods of northern Scotland. They have declined in recent years and now number fewer than 2,000 birds in the whole of Scotland. Part of a well-funded programme to revive capercaillie involves killing crows and foxes who prey on both chicks and adults. Do you agree with this action?

Yes 66%   No 25%   Don't know 9%

- I think resources would be better spent on protecting the capercaillies' natural habitat by restoring native pinewoods. That way they are addressing the cause rather than the symptoms.

- Predators should only be controlled when the species being protected is at an extremely low ebb, as is the case with the capercaillie.

- The problem is more about habitat destruction. Capercaillies thrive with these predators in Scandinavia.

- Capercaillie are a beautiful bird and hopefully killing crows will help considerably.

- Fox and crow numbers are out of control nationwide, a more co-ordinated effort should be made to control their numbers

- Instead of culling foxes and crows would it not be better to cull the number of deer to allow natural regeneration of woodland habitat?

- What contest is there between a Scottish emblem and vermin?

- If a creature cannot survive in an environment without significant assistance, sadly we must allow it to die out.

- Killing one species to support another is wrong, and comes back to our own aesthetics.

- We have a surfeit of crows and foxes because of the lack of top predators which we have wiped out. Until we restore the balance, we will need to control them.

- We need to accept that if the numbers of capercaillie can only increase due to Man's constant intervention by predator control then this is expensive and ultimately unsustainable.

- It is worth the culling of common animals in order to try and protect this flagship species.

- It is a highly inefficient use of the extremely limited funds available for conservation.

- If capercaillie can't survive in the presence of predators then there is likely to be a deeper problem.

- The money should be spent on improving habitat and educating people.

Pine martens are a rare member of the same family as stoats and are protected by law. Since being protected, they have increased in numbers across northern Scotland. They will eat almost anything from berries to carrion. Included in their diet are birds' eggs, mice, squirrels and recently they have been found to prey on a rare breeding duck called goldeneye. Pine martens will climb into the duck's nest and kill the incubating female and then eat the eggs. Do you think the law protecting pine martens should be changed to allow greater protection for their rare prey species?

Yes 40%   No 49%   Don't know 11%

- In the future pine martens will be like foxes, a nuisance that eat and kill everything for the sake of it.

- It doesn't take long after one of our most iconic predators dares to make a bit of a comeback before someone starts complaining about the fact that a predator has the bare-faced cheek to actually prey on things.

- Tough on the ducks but a female goldeneye only has to raise two young in her lifetime to replace herself and her mate.

- All wildlife has a right to survive and who is to say which species is more important.

- There HAS to be a balance in nature, the pine marten population is now out of control.

- Pine martens have declined dramatically in the last 100 years through human persecution, and should be allowed to develop naturally.

- They are cute and furry; our resident animal destroyed a siskin nest, but that's what happens. If only they would be more interested in collared doves.

- Whilst I believe in predator management, I believe the changing of the law would seriously threaten pine marten populations.

- Pine martens are still rare as a result of persecution. Goldeneye may be a rare UK breeder but are numerous in other countries.

- Goldeneye nest in artificial boxes. There must be a means of adapting them to restrict entry.

- Goldeneye is only rare here because it is a recent colonist. Pine martens are native. I think a balance will be reached.

- If they are predating too heavily in a given area on a given species, they must be controlled.

- They must only be controlled in areas where they prey on species as rare or rarer than themselves.

The fox hunting debate has been very public and continues to be contentious. Foxes are opportunist hunters and scavengers. They have a tendency to prey on domestic livestock and are often considered to be cruel and ruthless. Do you think fox numbers should be controlled?

Yes 56%   No 36%   Don't know 8%

- They need keeping down to protect game, which in turn creates work for keepers and keeps families in the countryside.

- The way to control them is the natural way, by re-introducing the other predators that belong here.

- I have lost several chickens to foxes over the years, but still am lost in admiration when I see one crossing my garden at dusk or dawn.

- It is essential to control fox numbers due to their slaughter of domestic fowl and because they potentially carry a number of diseases that are transmissible to humans and dogs.

- My local foxes are happy knowing I leave food out for them – it seems to work. My poultry roam free and I haven't lost any this year.

- If foxes are having a serious impact on endangered ground-nesting birds then limited control should be enforced.

- Farmers complain about foxes but often do not invest in fencing to adequately protect their livestock.

- Fox control needs to be done humanely. At present it seems that if you give an animal the 'vermin' label you don't need to worry about the welfare issues.

- Our local farmer is happy for foxes to breed on his land as they keep the rats and mice numbers in check.

- Only man is a cruel and ruthless animal – foxes are simply hungry.

- Fox numbers have boomed and now they are not being moved around by hunts they are a huge pest.

- In years of working on an upland sheep farm, I have seen many predated lambs but I am yet to see a fox kill a healthy lamb!

- Can people in towns be discouraged from feeding foxes – they aren't cute they are vermin – you wouldn't feed rats with a bowl of dog food.

- What a pity hunting was banned as it was one of a variety of methods of control which brought great economic benefit and enormous pleasure to thousands.

- Foxes are beautiful but ruthless. They must be controlled.

There are approximately nine million pet cats in the UK. Although they are domesticated, their natural instinct is to hunt for themselves and it is estimated that between them, they kill 270 million birds and small mammals each year. Would you support a nationwide legislative reduction in cat numbers?

Yes 60%   No 32%   Don't know 8%

- People acquiring cats need to be educated on their impacts and owners should be advised to neuter pets.

- I don't think that cats really affect bird populations and are useful for deterring rodents from entering houses.

- People seem to forget that when they buy that fluffy kitten, they're bringing a predator into their home.

- Cats provide a lot of pleasure to their owners and are only acting naturally.

- Cats are not native to the UK and people who keep them as pets should be forced to have them in their houses, not roaming around everyone else's property!

- I think that all households should be restricted to one cat, then the population would fall.

- I convinced my neighbour to fit loud falconry bells to her cats and the bird population in our garden has benefited.

- What about the studies that show the benefit of cats, as companion animals, in helping humans recover from illnesses?

- I have a cat and have seen the damage it can do to birds – no more cats in this house after this one dies.

- There is a very high feral cat population which should be eradicated for the sake of genuine Scottish wildcats.

- If someone's dog came into our gardens killing the wildlife we'd be up in arms, what makes cat owners think their pet is exempt from this?

- It is part of nature for cats to hunt. Nothing wrong with that. My cats often bring me 'presents'. Sometimes only the head!

- Why not introduce the necessity to have a licence to keep a cat, or put an 'environmental tax' on cats that can be used to improve habitat for wild birds.

- I have tried to curb my cat's hunting success (never very marked) by using a pump-action water pistol to disturb both cat and target. The cat has now given up hunting altogether.

White-tailed eagles have been reintroduced into Scotland after having been hunted to extinction in Victorian times. They are capable of preying on live lambs. As we consider further reintroductions elsewhere, do you think that farmers who suffer losses should be compensated?

Yes 63%   No 30%   Don't know 7%

- As the land owners/farmers hunted them to extinction in the first place I see no reason why they should be compensated.

- Farmers who have taken reasonable steps to protect their livestock from known predators yet still sustain losses should be compensated on our (the public) behalf.

- Predation by the magnificent white-tailed eagle should be seen by farmers as a normal part of the ongoing costs of running a livestock farming business.

- It isn't fair for the farming community to shoulder the financial burden of lambs becoming prey to these outstanding birds.

- If farmers are not compensated for losses to livestock they are liable to take the law into their own hands which will only be bad news for the eagles.

- The continued existence (and possible reintroduction) of predators in this country depends very much on the goodwill of the farming community.

- If this species has been reintroduced after a long absence, then those doing the reintroduction should be responsible for the financial consequences of their actions.

- Payment purely for loss of livestock is open to abuse and still maintains the belief that predators are damaging.

- It is very difficult to expect reintroduced species to live hand in hand with modern society.

- I live in an area where sea eagles regularly take live lambs, at some nests in quite large numbers. By compensating the farmers (which already happens in my area) we can ensure that the eagles are not persecuted.

- If we are serious about conservation, we need to be prepared to pay for it. This will help to keep public support for such schemes and the goodwill of farmers and landowners whose co-operation could be crucial.

- Here is an opportunity and an approach that would make the farmers involved support the eagles and see a value in their existence.

- The numbers taken by eagles are insignificant – I would consider it an honour to have one of my lambs taken by a sea eagle instead of the usual fox or a crow pecking its eyes out!

- Lamb losses are low in general but for individual farmers can be very significant.

Under the EU Habitats Directive, the British government is under an obligation to examine the feasibility of reintroducing those species that once lived here. Candidates include Eurasian lynx, wolf, wild boar and brown bear. Assuming appropriate habitat was available, which, if any, of these would you support?

Lynx	Yes **67%**	No **23%**	Don't know **10%**
Wolf	Yes **60%**	No **30%**	Don't know **10%**
Wild boar	Yes **67%**	No **23%**	Don't know **10%**
Brown bear	Yes **47%**	No **42%**	Don't know **11%**

- It would be lovely to think that the Scottish wilderness could support such species as lynx, wolf and bear but it is simply unrealistic – we live in too crowded a country.

- They manage to live with these species in other parts of Europe, so why not here?

- I don't think dangerous animals should be reintroduced.

- Nature has decreed that these species should not survive in this country. To reintroduce them would be a grave mistake.

- The pressures on our remaining species are growing, they should have priority.

- I support the reintroduction of top-level carnivores as I think that ecological health depends on their presence.

- These are all extinct in UK because of a 'risk' to animals, property or people. The UK is too small and overcrowded for them.

- I feel these 'headline' species detract from the endangered species that are present already, and from the real problem of habitat protection and management.

- In countries where both exist, there are few dangerous incidents between animals and Man. If introduced, we should educate the public about the animals and how to behave in areas where they live

- I think the UK is far too overpopulated to make it fair to reintroduce species with large territories. They would only come into contact with humans, who would somehow contrive to destroy them either through ignorance or for profit.

- I would support all if suitable habitats could be found but whatever happens, this should be done primarily in the interests of conservation and not for Man's entertainment.

- I think people would be very scared. It would be chaos. One human victim and every hunter would go on a massacre again. We can't do that to the animals AGAIN.

- In order to provide suitable habitat for the top predators and keystone species the whole ecosystem would have to be in excellent functioning condition.

Please choose which of these statements you most agree with:

1. **Humans have the right to manage all wildlife to suit our needs.**
2. **Some wildlife species should be controlled if they interfere with human activities.**
3. **Wildlife should not be managed by humans as nature will find its own balance.**

- Most human management of our wild animals is for selfish pleasure and greed.

- It is a mistake to think that our activities don't have an impact on all 'wild' species. Better to acknowledge our influence, seek to understand it and then make informed choices about what we do.

- Humans too are part of nature, so it's not actually practical to completely divorce ourselves from the issues. We do have to make some tough decisions.

- Wildlife cannot find a 'natural' balance – unless humans go back to living like cavemen.

- In today's society Man will always dominate over nature one way or the other.

- Human life and quality comes first but that need not be at the expense of all the other forms of life with which we share our planet.

- When managing all natural resources we should have a scientific rather than emotional approach.

- It goes without saying that certain species should be controlled where they interfere with human activities.

- We live in an artificial world and we must be able to control and manage all species.

- Clearly some animals such as deer will always have to be controlled unless we reintroduce their natural predators.

- Wildlife should be managed for their benefit first and foremost as their survival and welfare will ensure our own.

- We have reached a stage when we need to do proactive things to help wild animals and places, otherwise it will all be turned to concrete or a shopping mall.

- Humans seem to be preoccupied with changing the balance to suit their own needs and then wonder why animals become extinct. We share this planet...we do not own it.

- Animals should be controlled where they are a severe economic or health threat, not to increase the pleasure of people who prefer one wild species over another.

- We need to accept that the balance is never static – it constantly changes. This is evolution and extinctions are natural.

- Humans have changed the wild environment so much that we now have a DUTY to manage where appropriate to maximise biodiversity.

Other selected comments

- If every human lived the lifestyle of the average westerner we would need three planet earths to supply the resources! So if developing nations become 'developed' we are well and truly up the creek with no paddles and with a few holes in the hull as well.

- Nature does not need us, we need it.

- As a species and as top predator we have remained immune to the usual impact of predator upon prey and our numbers are not controlled by our prey species. That is why our population is out of control.

- Nature does not need laws to protect certain species. There is an ecology link that has been in place for centuries and we tamper with this at our peril.

- In today's environment we need to control aggressive species to achieve a balance!

- We simply do not have enough knowledge, scientific or otherwise, to be meddling in the processes of nature.

- To control one rare species for the benefit of another is a judgement that is beyond us both ethically and practically, and way beyond our understanding of ecology.

- Everything needs protecting from Man but not from each other.

- Unless we can learn to live beside predators and accept some competition, we will not learn how to live as part of ecosystems rather than outside them in the future.

- We are the planet's top predator, and if we can't give other predators room on this increasingly money-driven, overcrowded world, then we have reached a sad and morally reprehensible state of affairs.

- Wildlife should be managed where necessary to restore/maintain ecosystems.

- The fact that we have pets signifies a need in humans to have some contact or identification with animals.

- I think that to cull predators only displays a lack of understanding of the natural balance of nature.

- I find it curious that we love our pets so much and yet know very little about wild creatures. The wolf and the dog are very typical examples of this. We pamper our dogs, and yet persecute the wolf relentlessly.

- We live in a world where conservation is a luxury.

- The arrogance of humankind distresses me. It is time we found our rightful place in the circle of life and stopped trying to control everything.

- How can the most unmanaged animal ever to exist be so arrogant as to think it has the right or knowledge to manage the very system that produced it!

"WHEN ONE TUGS AT A SINGLE THING IN NATURE, HE FINDS IT ATTACHED TO THE REST OF THE WORLD."

JOHN MUIR

THANKS!

Since the inception of the *Tooth & Claw* project, we have received an enormous amount of help from a huge range of individuals and organisations. Without you the project would simply not have been possible. If we didn't thank you at the time, we hope that we have managed to do so below and we apologise sincerely if we've missed anyone out. The assistance and information freely given represents a genuine desire on the part of the majority of contributors to ensure a healthy future for Britain's predators.

Tooth & Claw would not exist were it not for the unconditional support of family and friends to whom we owe an enormous debt of gratitude.

Special thanks to: Amanda, Sam and Gale.

And...

Alladale Wilderness Reserve	Maureen Dehany	Bob Kindness	Amie Proom
Alvie Estate	Kevin Deignan	Simon King	Ilka Reinhardt
Zanete Andersone-Lilley	Roy Dennis	Gesa Kluth	Jessica Richards
Helen Armour	Derby Museum & Art Gallery	Jake Knight	John Robbins
Nigel Atkinson	Raymond Dingwall	Andy Langley	Donnie Ross
Ed Bangs	Catriona, Lesley and Fiona	Daniel Lee	Iain Ross
Allan Bantick	Dudgeon	Paul Lister	Bill Rowlands
BBC Wildlife magazine	Andrew Dixon	Jani Maatta	Jana Schellenberg
Troy Bennett	The Dixon family	David MacDonald	Lee Schofield
Niall Benvie	Iain Erskine	Peter MacDonald	Dave Sexton
Johnny Birks	Brian Etheridge	Thomas MacDonnell	Victoria Sims
Stewart Blair	Alan Watson Featherstone	Cynthia and Alec MacFadyen	Gill Sinclair
Steve Bottom	Anke Fischer	Ann Mackay	Colin Sheddon
Ian Boyd	Tracy Fleming	Ramsay Mackay	Toni Shelbourne
Jill Brown	Billy Forbes	Daska Mackintosh	Adam Smith
Nic Brown	Andrew Ford	Phillip MacLeod	Doug Smith
Tommy Bryce	Hugh Fullerton-Smith	Innes MacNeill	Nigel Smith
Gordon Buchanan	Colin Galbraith	John MacPherson	Melanie Smith
Burt Burnett	Martin Gaywood	Keith Marshall	Robin Smith-Ryland
British Wildlife Centre	Helen Gillies	Bradley Mayo and Parents	Murray Stark
Calumet Photographic	Stuart Glen	Ronnie McLeod	Anita Szon
Mark Cawardine	George Gow	Robert Melrose	Denise Taylor
Iain Cadzow	Isla Graham	Rick Minter	Simon Thorp
Matthew Capper	Mike Groves	Rima Morrell	Mike Towler
David Clark	Duncan Halley	Keith Morton	Bill Tucker
Louise Clark	Tony Hamblin	Nick Moyes	Jill Tyson
Peter Collins	Val Hamblin	Jorg Muller	Staffan Widstrand
Richard Cooke	Josh Hambry	Carl Neumann	Sarah Williams
Combe Primary School	Rob Harris	Frank Neumann	Gerry Wilson
Roz Kidman Cox	Anne Haddow	Duncan Orr-Ewing	Paul Winter
Tony Crease	Hessilhead Wildlife Hospital	Tsa Palmer	David Woodhouse
Peter Cunningham	David Hetherington	Mike Park	Helen Woodward
Ole Martin Dahle	Highland Wildlife Park	Allan & Morag Paul	Sam Wrigley
Adrian Davis	Kate Jack	Peterhead Fish Market	Alison Young
George Davis	Jacqui Kaye	Chris Powell	Zoe and Josh
Tom Dawson	Andy Keen	David Power	

PETER CAIRNS

Based in the heart of Scotland's Cairngorms National Park, Peter Cairns is a freelance nature photographer with a deep fascination for our relationship with the natural world. In addition to documenting Europe's high-profile wildlife species, his work focuses on a diverse range of issues such as wildlife management, ecological restoration, eco-tourism and evolving land-use regimes. In *Tooth & Claw*, the realisation that wildlife politics is not about wildlife but about us, comes to the fore.

www.northshots.com

MARK HAMBLIN

Mark is an award-winning wildlife and landscape photographer supplying stock images to international photographic agencies, as well as running his own library. He writes and illustrates features for a number of photographic and countryside magazines and has published two previous books, *Wild Peak* and *Wild Land*. Mark is also a partner in Wildshots, leading photo-tours in Scotland and overseas.

www.markhamblin.com

PHOTOGRAPHIC CREDITS

Peter Cairns 10, 14(all), 15(all), 16(all), 17, 19(all), 20, 21, 27(all), 38/39, 43, 44, 46, 52, 53, 54, 55, 56, 57, 58/59, 61, 62, 63, 65, 67, 68, 69, 70, 72, 75, 82(all), 83 (top), 87, 105, 107, 111, 112, 113, 114, 117, 119, 120 (r), 121, 123, 125, 126, 128, 136, 138, 147, 148/149, 150, 153, 154, 155, 159, 160, 161, 166, 169, 170, 171, 173, 178, 180, 181, 183, 184, 185(all), 186/187, 188, 190, 192, 193, 194, 195, 199, 200, 201(all), 202, 204, 205, 206, 210(all), 211, 213, 214, 218.

Mark Hamblin Cover, 7, 11, 12, 22, 24, 28, 30, 31, 32, 33, 34, 35, 36, 37, 47, 49, 50, 60, 74, 76, 77, 78/79, 81, 83 (btm), 84, 86, 88, 89, 90, 93, 94, 96, 97, 98, 99, 100, 101, 103, 104, 108, 109, 110, 116, 120 (lt & lb), 122, 124, 127, 129, 131(all), 132, 133, 134, 139, 140, 141(all), 142, 143, 145, 152, 157, 158, 162, 164, 165, 168, 172, 175(all), 176, 196, 208/209, 212, 215, 217, 220, 233.

Tony Hamblin 177.

Nick Moyes 115.